OAK LAWN PUBLIC LIBRARY

3 1186 00520 1066

W9-BYL-061

GREENHOUSE BASICS

Gardening in
Your Greenhouse

Mark Freeman

Illustrations by Heather Bellanca

STACKPOLE
BOOKS

0 11557 02776 1

APR 1 3 1999
OAK LAWN LIBRARY

To Mary Louise Freeman-Lynde, better known as Molly,
who has her great-grandmother's green thumb.

Copyright © 1998 by Mark Freeman

Published by
STACKPOLE BOOKS
5067 Ritter Road
Mechanicsburg, PA 17055

All rights reserved, including the right to reproduce this book or portions thereof
in any form or by any means, electronic or mechanical, including photocopying,
recording, or by any information storage and retrieval system, without permission
in writing from the publisher. All inquiries should be addressed to Stackpole
Books, 5067 Ritter Road, Mechanicsburg, Pennsylvania 17055.

Printed in the United States of America

10 9 8 7 6 5 4 3 2 1

FIRST EDITION

Cover design by Wendy Reynolds
Cover line drawing by Heather Bellanca
Cover photo by Anne B. Freeman
Turf-Spray Home and Garden Sprayer Model 2501 in cover potograph used with
permission of Chapin Manufacturing, Inc.
The logos on the illustration on page 73 used with permission of Bentley Seeds Inc.,
Charles C. Hart Seed Co., and Shepherd's Garden Seeds

Library of Congress Cataloging-in-Publication Data

Freeman, Mark, 1927–
    Gardening in your greenhouse / Mark Freeman ; illustrations by Heather
    Bellanca — 1st ed.
        p.   cm. — (Greenhouse basics)
    Includes index.
    ISBN 0–8117–2776–9
    1. Greenhouse gardening. 2. Greenhouses. I. Title. II. Series: Freeman,
Mark, 1927– Greenhouse basics.
SB415.F 74   1998
635.9'823—dc21
                                                                    98-4842
                                                                         CIP

Contents

Preface

I live and garden some thirty miles from Bennington, Vermont, at an elevation approximately 600 feet above sea level. The U.S. government says we are in Growing Zone 4; in general I agree. The average dates of last and first frosts here are May 10 and September 20, which gives us a growing season of 132 days. Our average annual percentage of possible sunshine is 53; in the three darkest months (November through January), we receive only 43 percent of possible sunshine.

In discussing greenhouse, and some outdoor, gardening conditions in this book, I have tried to allow for those who live in milder or harsher climates, but you may have to adjust some of my advice to make it applicable to your climate. To find out what zone you live in, check a good gardening encyclopedia; some seed catalogs also contain zone information.

To find out about your local *insolation,* which is the percentage of possible sunshine that you receive each month, see chapter 14. A good almanac, like the *Old Farmer's Almanac,* will tell you how many hours of sunlight are possible on any given day where you live, or at least at the nearest large city. If you've had a solar home or greenhouse for several years, you may already have a gut feeling for this; for example, we've known for years that it's really dark here in November but that we get a lot of sunlight in February.

SOME NOTES ON STYLE

The "editorial we" used to have a purpose, in that it added some dignity to a piece of written work. Now, when every semieducated pro athlete and race car driver uses it, as in "We are going to examine all our options before we decide to sign the contract," it cries out for the response "Have you got a frog in your pocket?" The author prefers the straightforward *I*. Where *we* is used in this book, it refers to some group of people, often but not always the author and his family.

I have found no good term in common use for home greenhouse owners. For this reason, I have coined the word *greenhousers* for those who own and work in a noncommercial greenhouse. It is a homely word, but it serves the purpose.

I have tried to use common names for plants in this book, with certain exceptions. In discussing vegetables, I use terms such as brassica and Solanaceae to avoid the vaguer terms "cabbage types," which some might not know includes turnips, and "tomato family," which also includes peppers and eggplants. I have given the Latin as well as the common names for all houseplants because they have a bewildering variety of common names. For example, what you may know as Patient Lucy somebody else calls Busy Lizzie. In many cases, such as coleus, the Latin name also is the common name.

All temperatures mentioned in this book are Fahrenheit. I have nothing against progress, but I have yet to meet a greenhouser in the United States who uses a Celsius thermometer, and a good many Canadians I know are just as comfortable with Fahrenheit as Celsius. If you aren't, I apologize, but you'll just have to use a conversion table.

If by any chance you are reading this book before constructing your own home greenhouse, I urge you to read the earlier book in this series, *Greenhouse Basics: Building Your Own Greenhouse,* because many of the ideas that follow work best in a greenhouse built according to the principles in that book.

I want to thank Laura McDermott, mentor of the Washington County Master Gardeners, and all the Master Gardeners who helped me with information and advice, especially Debbie Bailey. John Gail of Stokes Seeds provided a great deal of information about vegetable varieties for greenhouse growing, and Tim Kavanaugh of Rice Seeds helped me understand the seed industry in general and the problems of small seed companies in particular. Mike Taylor taught me a lot about houseplants and their use in large public buildings like hotels.

I could not have written this book, or anything else, without the help of my wife, Anne, who criticizes (in the true sense), corrects, proofreads, folds and staples, but does not mutilate, and is the world's best speller.

Introduction

Although you wouldn't know it from the mass media, as we enter the twenty-first century the fastest-growing recreational activity in America may be—not playing with a home computer—but gardening. Growing things in the backyard has always been a popular activity, and a necessity for some, but gardeners today are branching out into areas regarded as exotic by many a generation ago.

There are gardening books less than twenty-five years old that recommend the use of large quantities of DDT and other poisons as the solution to all pest problems. Today it is not necessary to identify oneself as an organic gardener; those who do not use compost and other natural fertilizers or who try to control pests and diseases with chemicals are now considered to be the oddballs, as organic gardeners were a quarter century ago.

In addition to practicing organic gardening, the majority of today's gardeners seek out plants and growing systems long considered exotic. Who today doesn't grow leeks and cilantro? Who doesn't know about raised beds and no-till systems? Herbs like rosemary and tarragon are common in home gardens; to be unusual today, you have to grow hyssop and lovage.

Granted, some home herb growing, like some "organic" gardening, is a fad, but there is a large core of determined gardeners who simply have found that herbs make food taste better—and may do at least as much for your health as the cold remedies and antacids found in drugstores. They like the taste of plum tomatoes and blue potatoes. They have found through trial and error that ladybugs control aphids better than malathion does and that cow manure is superior to 5–10–5 from a factory. And they're not about to go back to the old ways.

And then there's greenhousing. It began because many of us lived too far north to start tomatoes from seed outdoors or to eat lettuce out of the garden in December. We bought tomato and pansy plants at the local supermarket in the spring, tomatoes and lettuce at the same place in the winter. The taste of the produce didn't compare with what we grew ourselves, in season, and we discovered that what we ate, as well as the plants we bought to set out, had been liberally laced with chemicals. Besides, even the garden supply stores didn't sell Principe Borghese tomato plants, and the supermarket lacked arugula. (That last is only partly true today, when every small-town supermarket has exotic produce unknown to our parents, but we still don't know what it's been sprayed with.)

Perhaps no aspect of gardening is growing faster than the use of the home greenhouse. There are no reliable statistics on it, for the most part because an unknown but very large number of home greenhouses have been built, not by professionals or from kits, but from scratch by owners or neighborhood handymen, using guides like the author's *Greenhouse Basics: Building Your Own Greenhouse* (Stackpole Books, 1997). There may be as many as a million home greenhouses in the United States and Canada. They range from glorified glassed-in window boxes to conservatories on great estates.

This book is intended for the home greenhouse owner or those thinking about becoming one. It provides all the basic information needed for the activities most home greenhouse owners engage in: starting seeds, raising houseplants, and growing food and flowers for personal consumption. A final section deals with some unusual uses some people have made of their greenhouses, from drying herbs to frolicking in a hot tub.

In my experience, the most common use of a home greenhouse is for starting seedlings for later transplanting into the outdoor garden. The second most common use is for growing houseplants such as geraniums or aloes during all or most of the year. For many greenhouse owners, these plants may include a miniature orange tree or a pot of basil, but only a very few grow food or flowers for their own consumption on any scale larger than that. It's impossible to say how many make "unusual" uses of their greenhouses and what all of those might be. You don't even want to think about it; after all, the greenhouse is a warm and sunny place.

The organization of this book reflects the above distribution of uses. After a section on matters that all growers must be concerned with, such as soils, water, and ventilation, there is a fairly extensive discussion of starting seedlings, a considerable amount of information on houseplants, a short section on growing food, and a very brief section on uses of the greenhouse that have little or nothing to do with green plants.

This book is *not* intended for commercial growers, orchid fanciers, or experts in the cultivation of exotic cacti, bromeliads, bamboos, African violets, or other unusual specimens. If you are one of the above, you know a lot more about your specialty than I do. Maybe you can pick up a few tips here, maybe not, but please don't write the publisher to tell him that I don't know diddly about orchids. He and I already know that.

PART I

General Greenhouse Information

Types of Greenhouses and Their Uses

*A*lways and *never* are two words that should always be avoided and never used, especially by a writer on gardening subjects. It is true, however, that greenhouses almost always fall into one of two categories: attached or freestanding. Which kind you have, or plan to have, will be the principal factor in determining when you use your greenhouse, what you grow in it, and how much it costs you to build and maintain it.

I am speaking, of course, of home greenhouses. Commercial greenhouses are more difficult to categorize, since most commercial growers have a number of greenhouses, usually attached to each other directly or through a passage room, and attached eventually to an office or salesroom. Such greenhouses are carefully (and expensively) heated, cooled, and ventilated, which is why Valentine's Day roses cost so much.

FREESTANDING GREENHOUSES

Freestanding greenhouses, as the name implies, are not attached to any building, but stand alone. They are almost always built adjoining or near the home garden. Sometimes they are smack in the middle of it. They are usually built of inexpensive materials by the owner or a local handyman. The most popular framing material is polyvinyl chloride (PVC) pipe, more commonly used for plumbing. A PVC pipe greenhouse is almost always glazed with thin clear plastic, called *6-mil*. Sometimes a double thickness of 6-mil is used. This glazing material is sturdier than it looks and has the further advantage that when it tears or otherwise deteriorates after three to five years, it can be quickly, easily, and cheaply replaced.

Fig. 1. A freestanding greenhouse with one end partitioned off as a tool-shed.

Occasionally, freestanding greenhouses are more permanent structures, with wooden or steel framing and glass, fiberglass, or acrylic glazing. Such a structure may have a concrete foundation (PVC greenhouses usually just sit on the ground) and be insulated below ground. Whatever material it is made of, it usually is "all glass"—that is, the glazing material extends to the ground. Such a greenhouse is almost always rectangular; sometimes the short sides are opaque.

A freestanding greenhouse is suitable only for extending the growing season by a couple of months in the spring and the fall, unless the owner is willing to spend a great deal of money on heat and light, as commercial growers do. Without artificial heat, nighttime temperatures inside a freestanding greenhouse will be only a few degrees warmer than outdoors.

This does not mean that such a structure is not useful. In Zone 4, for example, a freestanding greenhouse can be used from about mid-March to late November. Seeds can be started in the greenhouse or, as is more commonly done, can be started in a warm basement or other part of the house, under lights, and the plants moved out to the greenhouse in March or April. When there is a threat of frost, a small, inexpensive heater can be turned on, manually or thermostatically.

Plants can be moved into such a greenhouse when frost threatens in the fall, or they can be started there in August or September. Some plants that will stand quite a bit of cold, like broccoli, lettuce, or pansies, will thrive in this environment until mid-December or later. Usually it is not the cold, but the shortness of the days, that ends their growth.

Oddly, more plants die in freestanding greenhouses from heat than from cold. Most greenhousers are alert to the possibility of frost, but it is hard to believe that at ten o'clock on a sunny spring morning, when the thermometer dropped to 28 the night before, the temperature inside the freestanding greenhouse is 130 degrees. Freestanding greenhouses need ventilation, and plenty of it. This is often provided by arranging the thin plastic walls so that they can be rolled up from the bottom 3 feet or more on all sides.

MODIFIED FREESTANDING GREENHOUSES

If you are a really determined member of the back-to-the-earth movement, you can grow some crops almost all year round in an unheated modified freestanding greenhouse, such as the one well-known homesteaders Helen and Scott Nearing built on the coast of Maine. Modifications include digging the greenhouse several feet into the earth to take advantage of ambient earth temperatures and backing it up to a stone wall or earth bank on the north side.

This provides a sort of cross between a freestanding and an attached greenhouse. In it, depending on the harshness of your climate, you can grow certain hardy crops almost all winter long, mostly cabbages and mustards of Asian origin. The usefulness of such a greenhouse will be increased by a system of blankets or shutters that can be put into use at night to retain some of the daytime heat.

There are a number of greenhouses, usually homemade, that are attached not to a dwelling but to an outbuilding. Unless the outbuilding is heated, these usually function more like freestanding than like attached greenhouses, but there can be advantages in this arrangement. The north wall of the greenhouse can be insulated, and the outbuilding can provide storage for greenhouse tools and materials, leaving all the greenhouse space for growing plants.

ATTACHED GREENHOUSES

If the above seems like more work than you wish to engage in, or if you want to grow something more than cabbage in the cold months or have a place to store fragile houseplants in winter, you need an attached greenhouse. The traditional conservatory and sunporch are both examples of attached greenhouses.

For some curious reason, the modern attached greenhouse is often referred to as a "solar greenhouse," as though freestanding greenhouses received their heat and light from some source other than the sun. A better term might be "partial greenhouse," as it is attached to some other structure and thus at least one side is opaque. In addition, many attached greenhouses have no glazing, or only a few skylights, in the roof. Most attached greenhouses are attached to the south side of a home to provide protection from the cold north winds of winter. Conservatories made almost entirely of glass may be found in England, where the climate is milder, as extensions on the east or west ends of mansions.

Attached greenhouses, unlike freestanding ones, are almost always built of sturdy, relatively expensive materials. Often they are built by professionals, either when the house is first constructed or as a later addition. There is usually insulation under the floor, which is often made of slate or bricks. Glazing is often double-pane glass. The roof may not be glazed at all or may have a few skylights. Areas that are not glazed are heavily insulated. Most attached greenhouses have electricity, running water, and a drain or drains.

Fig. 2. An attached greenhouse provides an additional room off the living room of this solar home.

Attached greenhouses usually incorporate *heat sinks*. A heat sink consists of a large amount of dense material that absorbs energy slowly when it is heated and returns the stored energy slowly when the surrounding area is cooled—in other words, a material into which heat can be "sunk." The two most popular heat-sink materials are water and masonry: brick, sand, stone, and mortar. Through a careful balance of glazed and insulated areas and a judicious use of heat-sink material, you can create a sunspace in which you can live year-round as well as grow plants, one that will provide your home with a net heat gain, although you may have to heat it artificially during the darkest weeks of the year. Usually all the heat necessary can be provided simply by opening the doors and vents between the greenhouse and the rest of the house.

If you are contemplating building an attached greenhouse, I recommend having little or no glazing in the roof. Because of the angle at which sunlight reaches the ground in the cold months, an attached greenhouse with plenty of glazing in the south wall and some in the east and west walls will be reasonably warm in winter but not too hot in summer, especially if roof overhangs shade the south glass. A sunspace with a glazed roof will not be inhabitable in summer—by plants or by people—without an extensive ventilation system that essentially makes it part of the outdoors.

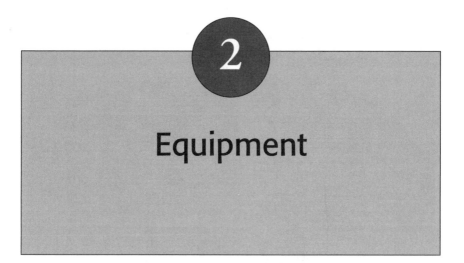

Equipment

Some greenhouses, though not many, have dirt floors. These may be simply the ground over which the attached or, more likely, freestanding greenhouse was pitched, like a tent. In a few cases, the greenhouse has a fairly deep and well-insulated foundation, which was filled with garden soil carried in from outside in an early phase of construction. Here the greenhouser probably intended from the beginning to raise plants in the floor.

More commonly, plants grow in beds, flats, or pots raised some distance from the floor. There are several good reasons for this. To begin with, the floor is generally the coldest place in any structure. Second, for good structural reasons, many greenhouses have knee walls, with the glazing beginning 3 feet or so off the ground. This means that plants on the floor close to the wall would receive little light. Finally, and perhaps most important, working with plants at waist level or higher helps the gardener avoid back problems.

It may be argued that the common arrangement of growing plants on raised surfaces wastes the space below the shelves or benches. In most greenhouses, however, this is used as storage space for the myriad pots, flats, tools, soil mixes, and other items necessary to horticulture.

BENCHES AND SHELVES

Most greenhousers raise plants on benches or shelves. Shelves are defined here as growing areas permanently attached to the greenhouse wall;

Fig. 3. Against the knee wall, under the glazing, is a great place to store greenhouse necessities. This greenhouser has cut a hole in a shelf to make more room for a tomato plant.

benches are shelves on legs. Shelves typically are attached at the top of the knee wall immediately under the glass; in some cases, the shelf may serve as or lie over a windowsill. Shelves below the top of the knee wall are handy places to store stuff, and nobody, be it greenhouser or house-holder, ever has too much storage space. Shelves are usually one above the other; careful design will ensure that an upper shelf doesn't shade a lower shelf. Plants that don't need total sun can be placed on lower shelves.

Most shelves are made of wood; a few greenhouses have shelves made of glass, fiberglass, or clear plastic. What you gain in light transmission by such an arrangement is generally counterbalanced by what you lose in expense, breakability, and the need for constant cleaning. If your shelves are packed as full as most greenhousers', not much light is going to get through anyway.

Benches can be as rough or as fancy as you please. A common kind of bench has legs made of wooden 2x2's or 2x4's and a rough wooden frame-work. The top can be made of plywood or boards, but because of the importance of good air circulation and drainage, it is more commonly made of a material that will let air and water through. Typical bench surfaces are hardware cloth or other wire grating material; less commonly seen, but cheap and serviceable, is scavenged snow fencing (*scavenged* here doesn't mean stolen from the town highway department, however).

THE POTTING BENCH

Every good greenhouse has a potting bench or table. You can make one about as easily as you can buy one, and certainly more cheaply. You will want to be able to work at it sometimes standing up, so make it the right height for that, then get a stool high enough that you can work at it sitting down as well. If you stand up all the time, your feet will hurt at the end of a session, and if you have to bend over much, your back will hurt as well. Incidentally, all plant benches should be about the same height as the potting bench, for the same reasons.

The potting bench should be quite large, perhaps 5 feet long by 3 feet wide. It should get plenty of natural light but might have a fluorescent light over it as well. After all, you won't always be potting, and the potting table may double as a germination table. It doesn't need to have a built-in sink, but water should not be far off. You may want to attach a short length of hose to the greenhouse faucet and lead it to the potting table, shutting it off there with a nozzle. The potting bench, unlike other

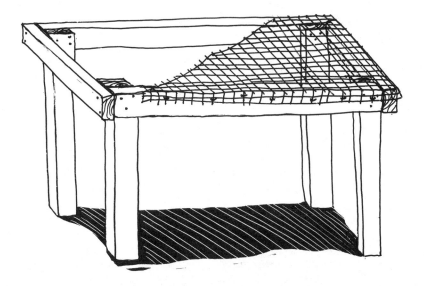

Fig. 4. A typical greenhouse bench, with hardware cloth top. Top is cut away to show construction.

greenhouse benches, should have a solid top. It is helpful if it has a large tray on it, covering one-half to two-thirds of the available surface.

TRAYS

How do shelves, as opposed to benches, provide water drainage? The answer has to do with the types of greenhouses that have shelves as opposed to benches, the watering systems employed in them, and the use of trays.

Visit a local commercial greenhouse, if you haven't already done so. In most cases, it is freestanding, with a roof that is either curved like a Quonset hut or peaked. Walls and roof are usually made of two layers of clear plastic with an air space between them. There are very large and expensive heaters and ventilators, and an overhead, probably automated watering system.

In such a greenhouse, every possible square foot is crammed with plants, but even here, there are no plants on the floor (except for the occasional pre–Mother's Day emergency). Plants are on benches like those described above. Aisles between benches are extremely narrow. The floor is gravel or some material that drains well.

Contrast this with a typical attached hobby greenhouse. It functions as a conservatory, a room in which plants can be grown in abundance, but nonetheless a room in a home. The floor is brick, slate, or tile. It has a drain but is not designed to always be wet. The glazing is less total than in the commercial example and is usually double-thick glass. Heat comes primarily from the sun and from the rest of the house, which is accessible through one or more double doors.

In such a structure, although a few plants may be on benches, most are on shelves, and neither the shelves nor the benches drain. Instead, large, sturdy trays of metal—galvanized, aluminum, or stainless steel—cover the entire surface of each shelf or bench, or at least a major portion. The tray has four upturned edges so constructed that it will hold 2 to 3 inches of water. Such a tray cannot be bought; it must be built.

In most towns, some large hardware store or construction supply store carries sheet metal. Although sheets of plywood are always 4 by 8, for some unknown reason sheets of metal are usually 3 by 8. Most such stores carry stainless steel, aluminum, and galvanized steel sheets. Stainless steel is sturdy, hard to bend, lasts just about forever, looks good, and costs the moon. Aluminum is easy to bend, lightweight, doesn't last as long or look as good as you thought it would, and costs half the moon. Good-quality galvanized steel is lowest in cost and medium in bendability, durability, and looks. We have galvanized trays in our greenhouse that are more than ten years old. They don't leak and have minuscule rust spots, if any. Every time we remember the price, they look pretty good. Any other metal is out of the question unless you own a copper mine. Galvanized steel can be made more attractive by painting, but that adds to the cost, involves at least two cumbersome coats, and readily chips off. Ours are unpainted.

To make a tray, measure the surface to be covered. Cut a piece of metal 2 to 3 inches larger all the way around. (For example, if the surface is 72 inches by 24 inches, cut a sheet 77 by 29.) Put the metal on the floor and bend up each edge the required amount. Bend it around a 2x4. A rubber hammer, like those used in auto body shops, and very strong fingers are useful for this. You'll soon get the hang of it; it *can* be done. You may want to use a nail to scribe a line on the metal where you want the bend.

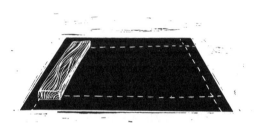

Fig. 5. The first step in making a greenhouse tray from a piece of sheet metal.

Fig. 6. Folding up the edges of a greenhouse tray.

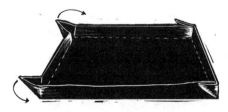

Fig. 7. Making "hospital corners" on a tray.

Corners are slightly more difficult; make "hospital corners," as when making a bed. They may not be perfect, but if the edge is bent up 2 1/2 inches all around, the corners will probably be high enough that the tray will hold 2 inches of water. A corner makes a handy spout when you want to drain water from the tray, and you *will* want to drain water from the tray.

The trays go on the shelves, directly under the window or glazing. The plants are grown in boxes, flats, pots, six-packs, or what-have-you that rest on the trays, not in the trays themselves. The water that drains out of the flats will evaporate from the surface of the tray, not rot the shelf or stay around the plant roots so long that your petunias suffer from "wet feet."

If you haven't yet built your shelves, slope them *slightly* toward the glass. This will give them a little more direct sunlight and also cause surplus water to flow to the edge of the tray. The evaporation of excess water will help increase the humidity in the greenhouse.

PLANTING CONTAINERS

Flats

Flat, in this book, is a term applied to a rectangular container with more than one pocket or cell; ideally there will be a plant in each pocket. Six-packs are the industry standard, but flats range from two- or conceivably one-pocket ones to those having 512 or more very tiny cells. Chapter 8 has detailed descriptions of several particularly useful sizes.

Usually, seeds are started in small-celled flats and seedlings are later moved to larger flats or, more commonly, pots. You can buy flats and pots, but I wouldn't worry about this. A greenhouse is like a pickup truck; once friends and even casual acquaintances find out you have one, they'll want to borrow it. (Unlike the pickup truck, the greenhouse must be used on your premises, but you'll find the borrowing just as much of a nuisance.) In return, they'll inundate you with secondhand flats and pots.

Pots

If you've done much indoor gardening, you've already decided about clay versus plastic, and nothing I say will change your mind, but I'll say it anyway. Clay pots cost much more and break much more easily, and plants in them require much more watering. They "breathe," which is one of the things purists like about them. The other argument is that they are "prettier," or at least more classic or natural looking. I say beauty is in the eye of the beholder, handsome is as handsome does, and if clay pots are so pretty, why do florists always cover them with colored foil?

Here's a tip I got from a commercial grower: If you are determined to use clay pots, spray the insides with shellac, and you won't need to water them so often. The bottom holes will provide enough drainage. You can achieve the same effect by lining each pot with clear plastic sandwich wrap (punch a hole in the bottom of the lining).

Another kind of pot is made of peat, somehow compressed to hold together (usually for a shorter time than you would have wished). Peat pots are often recommended for starting plants like cucurbits (squash, cucumbers, and similar plants) that are said to be hard to transplant. Theoretically, you put the plant in the garden, pot and all, and the roots find their way through the decaying pot. In practice, I have found that peat pots decompose only when you don't want them to, never after being set into the garden, and roots have a very hard time getting through them. Start your cucurbits in plastic pots as described in chapter 8.

Garden suppliers also sell various fancy seed-starting gizmos that are supposed to be potting soil and small pot all in one. They are seldom worth what they cost and have a nasty habit of drying out.

You might want to have a few fancy ceramic or china pots on hand to use for gifts. Grow the plant as described in later chapters and transplant it into such a pot a week or two before you give it away. In buying such pots, be sure that they have some kind of drainage holes. Hard as it is to believe, some manufacturers produce them without. A plant in a pot with no drainage will always die, sooner or later.

Styrofoam Containers

If your friends don't inundate you with flats and pots, you can buy a few to start with at a garden supply store, or you can use Styrofoam containers. Styrofoam is considered environmentally incorrect, but once the containers have been made and used for some other purpose, it does no harm, only good, to use them again.

Many chicken farmers have gone back to cardboard egg boxes, but if you can find any styrofoam ones, they are almost as good as small-celled flats for starting seeds. Usually they have a flat top and a bottom with twelve pockets. Cut them in half with a razor-blade knife and use both halves, even though the bottom works better. Seal holes and slots with masking tape, and be sure to punch lots of drainage holes with an ice pick.

Fig. 8. A Styrofoam egg carton, if you can find one, makes a good seed-starting flat.

Places that have coffee hours, such as offices or churches, will almost always give you their used Styrofoam cups free, once they have overcome the traditional hostility to people who want to scrounge in garbage pails. So will fast-food chains, but the local manager will be even more suspicious. Styrofoam cups are excellent receptacles for transplants, but they have certain drawbacks. They have to be washed thoroughly, they have to be punched with an ice pick, and worst of all, they have a terrible tendency to topple over, which can be counteracted only by cramming them into a homemade wooden box of the proper size.

Very Large Pots

If you are going to grow food for eating or flowers for cutting in the greenhouse, you will need either large pots or beds. Tomatoes, cucumbers, and similar plants can be grown in pots about the size of 5-gallon plastic pails. In fact, you can use 5-gallon plastic pails as pots. These can be obtained from farmers and other workers, but the best source is a Sheetrock taper; a busy one goes through five hundred or more pails of compound in the course of a year, and the residue in his discarded pails, unlike paint, is very easy to clean out. In addition to being cleaned, the pails need to have drainage holes drilled in them; trying to punch them out, as with a nail, will crack them. You may or may not want to remove the bails (metal handles).

Cleaning Flats and Pots

If you are like most greenhousers, in a very few years your collection of containers in which to grow plants will number in the thousands. They just accumulate: Friends give them to you, casual acquaintances clean out their sheds and bring you hundreds of dirty cracked pots, and although you have a greenhouse, from time to time you'll succumb and buy a plant in a pot or six baby celeries in a flat. Cleaning this collection is the most arduous job on earth.

The first step is to throw away all those that have any imperfections. Be rigorous. Especially if they're made of that annoying incredibly thin plastic, pots with a tiny crack will fall apart just after you've put your precious rosemary seed into them. Throw away anything you know you're not going to use. After a few years, you will have developed potting routines, and you'll know you're never going to have a use for tiny black paper-thin one-cell flats or four-packs with very large cells.

Second, be quite firm in telling benefactors that though you'd love to have their cast-offs, you really must beg them to clean them thoroughly before giving them to you and to discard all the cracked or injured pots. This will result in about half the stuff you get having received a sketchy cleaning before it reaches you.

Even with steps one and two, however, you're just going to have to get around to that frightful cleaning job someday. After trying various techniques, I've found that the best place to clean pots is outdoors, and the best time a hot, sunny day. I use a hose and a kiddie pool. If you don't have a kiddie pool, consider buying one. They have lots of other uses, like dog washing, and are fairly inexpensive. You can use a big washtub, but it's not nearly as good.

If you're trying to clean several hundred pots at once, don't bother with amenities like soap. First, separate the stacked pots until you have

Fig. 9. It may look silly, but a kiddie pool is the best place to wash a large quantity of pots.

individuals littering the lawn. Then shake out all the dirt, leaves, and dead spiders you can. Next, place them, open side up, in the kiddie pool or washtub.

Now go away for a few days; maybe it will rain on them. Next, hit them with the hardest spray from the hose you can manage; they will instantly turn over. Hold them with one hand and use the hose with the other. You will, of course, be wearing an old bathing suit.

When the pots and flats dry a bit, you'll find that you have not removed nearly as much dirt as you thought; each still has to be scrubbed, or at least sloshed, with a rag, a brush, or your fingers. You'll soon resort to the last-named, holding the pot upright and rubbing the sides and bottom with one hand while manipulating the hose with the other.

The pots can be dried by first spreading them around on the lawn, bottom side up. After they have drained for a few sunny hours, put them right side up on a tarpaulin, deck, or patio. If the weather interferes, take mostly dry ones into the greenhouse and spread them out in the sunshine there. (There's no way you're going to wash pots in the spring; you'll be doing this in late summer or fall when the greenhouse is relatively empty.)

Many authorities recommend sterilizing pots in a very dilute solution of bleach or vinegar. If you have only twenty pots to clean, sterilization may be practical, but I always seem to have a few hundred dirty pots, and I haven't yet had a problem with plant diseases imported into the greenhouse by pots when I use the above method of cleaning. Sunlight is a powerful germ killer that never hurts plants. Too much bleach or vinegar could conceivably get into the soil.

BEDS

Even very large pots are unsuitable for certain crops you may want to grow in your greenhouse, such as radishes or turnips. For such crops you will have to have beds. Beds may be simply laid out in a dirt floor, as mentioned above, or they may be rectangular areas of soil contained within bricks or concrete blocks. If the beds are to be raised on benches or shelves, however, frequently the greenhouser will want to make them out of wood. Whatever a bed is made of, it goes without saying that the bottom of the bed must drain freely.

Scrap wood is obtainable from a variety of sources. Often factories or warehouses give away used pallets. The wood can be cut and nailed into boxes of the desired size and shape. Wood from which beds are made will rot in a few years, three or four at the most. The greenhouser has two choices: make beds out of treated wood or make new ones every few years.

What effect treated wood has on plants grown near it is still a very controversial subject. The most common chemicals used as wood preservatives include old-fashioned creosote and modern chemicals with names like copper naphthenate, pentachlorophenol, and chromated copper arsenate. All of these are powerful poisons designed to kill not only the fungi and bacteria that cause rot, but also insects.

One study seems to show that even after many years of use, these powerful chemicals had migrated from the wood into the soil a distance measured only in centimeters; other studies had conflicting results. I myself prefer the work of building new wooden beds every four or five years, or making beds of bricks or concrete blocks, to the risk of poisoning my plants or myself. It takes only a few minutes to slap together a bed out of scrap wood, and since I throw out the soil in the bed at least annually, it is no great trouble to examine and repair or replace the bed at that time.

OTHER EQUIPMENT AND TOOLS

Most things designed for use in the kitchen are very handy in the greenhouse. If the husband is a greenhouser, his wife knows where to look for her missing measuring spoons or cookie sheet. Normal gardening tools like watering cans are useful, but it is surprising how handy kitchen forks and spoons are. Strainers are necessary for obtaining fine soil for covering

Fig. 10. Kitchen utensils often make wonderful greenhouse tools.

Fig. 11. Filled with tepid water, a 1-gallon sprayer has a multitude of uses in the greenhouse. Filled with a dilute soap solution, it discourages many pests.

Fig. 12. A recycled glass cleaner bottle makes a fine mister in the greenhouse.

plants. A large, 1-gallon sprayer has many uses in the garden and greenhouse, but an empty glass cleaner bottle with a spray top is handier for misting plants.

Cookie sheets and similar flat objects are also very useful. They should be the kind with an edge turned up all around, so that they will hold a $^1/_2$ inch or so of water. My absolute favorite piece of equipment of this kind is a cookie sheet from a commercial bakery. It is about 2 by 3 feet, far too big to go into most home ovens, but great for carrying about four flats.

A greenhouse always contains various pails and buckets, but plastic dishpans or storage containers are also very convenient for holding soil mixes or a few inches of water for bottom watering.

Most gardening tools are too big to be used in the greenhouse, but you will have occasional use for a small trowel, hand fork, dibble, garden scissors (not grass shears), small pruning shears, and other similar items. You will soon learn which small garden tools are useful in the greenhouse. Unless you're doing some large-scale crop growing indoors, you'll use a kitchen fork more often than a garden fork and a tablespoon more than a trowel.

You will need a soil thermometer, perhaps more than one, a magnifying glass, funnels, an ice pick or two, indelible marking pens, pencils, notepads, various-size nails, toothpicks, small wooden skewers, lollipop sticks, tongue depressors, longer bamboo plant supports, a razor-blade knife, and hundreds of other items. You may not need or have access to skewers, sticks, and depressors, but the more of them you have, the happier you'll be. Sticks off trees won't do; believe me, they won't.

You'll need string, both stiff for hanging things like bags full of drying thyme and soft jute for tying stems to supports. Old torn-up pajamas will do as well as jute. Many books recommend old pantyhose; I find flannel or cotton easier to tear or cut and easier on the plants. Pantyhose material is so tough you can tow a broken-down car with it.

Sooner or later, almost everything from the workbench or desk will end up in the greenhouse, for a longer or shorter stay: hammers, even a small sledge, tin snips, large and small staplers, various saws, knives of all kinds, drills—everything. It's a good practice—in fact, an extremely necessary practice—to go through the greenhouse every two weeks or so and clear out all such items, returning them to where they belong.

SOIL SCREENS

The greenhouse should be equipped with at least three sizes of screens, and possibly four or five. The finest screens, which provide very fine soil for covering seeds, will be strainers you've scrounged from the kitchen. The larger sizes can be bought, for a hefty price, from one of those luscious garden supply catalogs, but they are better and vastly cheaper if you make them yourself.

Hardware cloth is the name hardware merchants give to the wire mesh they sell; it comes in many widths and meshes. The length is cut to suit the buyer. A screen made from $1/4$-inch mesh and another made from $1/2$-inch will be sufficient for most greenhouse needs.

To construct a screen, use sturdy scrap wood to make a frame that is slightly larger all around than the container in which you will keep the sifted soil. (Rule out round containers for this purpose.) Fasten the parts of the frame together with nails, screws, corrugated fasteners, or L-shaped steel reinforcement plates. Cut the hardware cloth with tin snips to the outer measurement of the frame. Use large staples from a heavy-duty carpenter's stapler to fasten the hardware cloth to the frame. You may want to reinforce them with occasional poultry wire staples (the smaller kind). When the screen wears out from hard use, and it will, make a new one.

LABELS AND MARKERS

Marking beds, flats, pots, and rows is a good deal easier in the greenhouse than out in the garden, but it's still difficult—not difficult to do the marking, but difficult to find labels that will not fade or come off. Most such materials sold in catalogs, such as the wire ones with the thin metal plates and a special scriber to write on them, are useless as well as expensive.

The first item needed is a really indelible pen with a fairly fine point. Soft pencil will do for some uses, but for most, find a laundry marker that is truly indelible. Nothing will tell you for sure but trial and error. For a surface to mark, nothing is better than masking tape

Fig. 13. Masking tape and a truly indelible marker are indispensable for labeling.

for flats and pots. If it is pressed firmly to a dry surface, it won't come off in water. In fact, it practically won't come off at all, which is its chief drawback. It's hard to get it off at best, but the longer you wait, the harder it gets, especially if it has been exposed to considerable solar heat.

If you don't care much about looks, you can just put new masking tape over old when you reuse flats and small pots. Masking tape won't stick well to Styrofoam. Write directly on Styrofoam cups and egg cartons, and cross out and relabel the next year or throw those containers away.

For markers to thrust into soil in pots or beds, like the neat, pretty ones that come from the florist, you

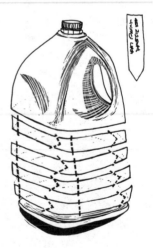

Fig. 14. The top of a plastic jug can protect young plants newly set out in the garden; the bottom can be cut up into handy markers.

can buy commercially made ones, of course, or you can use lollipop sticks or tongue depressors. Or you can make cheap, easy, convenient ones from a white plastic gallon or half-gallon jug that held bleach or some other liquid. The top half of the jug can be used to cover delicate plants when they are first set out (see chapter 10).

The bottom part, or the whole jug if you have a surplus, can be cut into plastic markers very easily, using sturdy garden scissors. Make them rectangular, of whatever size you need, such as 1 inch by 4 inches, and cut one end to a tapering point. Write on them with the laundry pen. They will stay legible unless they are sprinkled heavily and frequently with water, but when you want to reuse them, you can usually rub the marking off fairly well with a thumb. Of course, the ink won't come off your thumb so easily. Since they are easy and cheap to make, you may want to throw them away after one use.

There are dozens, if not hundreds, of items in addition to those mentioned here that you will find useful in the greenhouse. Most of them will have been intended by the manufacturer for some totally different use. You will learn over the years by trial and error just what they are and what use you can make of them.

Soil and Other Growth Media

Plants need air, water, food (nutrients), and, some say, love. This book says nothing about love, not because it's unimportant, but because it can't be taught. Air and water, closely interrelated, are discussed in the next chapter. The nutrients needed are in the soil or, if not, must be added by the gardener. It is not enough simply to add nutrients; they must be in a form the plant can readily use. If the soil is too clayey or too sandy, or if it contains too little humus, it will do little good, and may do harm, to apply a great deal of commercial chemical fertilizer to it. The plants will be unable to absorb most of the nutrients.

THE LIVING SOIL

What's the difference between soil and dirt? When the terms are used correctly, soil is alive, but dirt is dead. A cubic foot of garden soil might have a million living organisms in it. Most of these are microscopic or submicroscopic bacteria and other organisms. All bacteria ("germs") are not harmful; the vast majority are useful and necessary. To cite two examples, you couldn't digest food without the help of certain bacteria, and legumes like peas and beans couldn't fix nitrogen out of the air without others.

In addition to bacteria, the hypothetical cubic foot of soil would contain earthworms, the gardener's best friend; minuscule worms called nematodes; grubs; beetles, ants, and other insects too numerous to mention. It might contain a snake, a toad, a mole, or some other mammal. Most of these creatures are helpful to the gardener, or at least neither hurt nor help growing plants. Some nematodes attack plant roots; other nematodes attack the harmful nematodes.

There is not a great deal of difference, or there need not be, between the growing medium used in the greenhouse and that used in the outdoor garden. What difference there is comes about either because the gardener has the ability, because he is working with a much smaller quantity of soil, to exercise much more control over its characteristics (for example, he can make sure it doesn't contain moles) or because the primary use of soil in the greenhouse is for the starting of seeds and nurture of seedlings, and seeds always, and seedlings sometimes, have requirements different from those of mature plants, with regard to both structure and fertility.

PHYSICAL STRUCTURE OF SOIL

The structure of a soil is measured primarily by the size of the spaces within it. Think of concrete. One reason plants can't grow in it is that there are no spaces into which roots can expand or that can hold air or water. (Then think of how tough some trees are; their seeds can gain a foothold in the tiniest crack, and eventually their roots can split granite.) Coarse gravel is at the other extreme; spaces are large and numerous. Seedlings and some mature plants can't live in ordinary gravel because it drains too fast and contains few nutrients, but hydroponically grown vegetables, such as tomatoes, thrive when the fluid flowing through the gravel contains enough of the right nutrients and is maintained at exactly the correct level.

Soils are made up of clay, silt, sand, gravel, and humus. Most soils are a mixture of some or all of these, which (with the exception of humus) are listed in the order of particle size, clay having the finest particles. Size of particles determines size of spaces between particles.

One authority says that an ideal soil mix would be 40 percent sand, 40 percent silt, and 20 percent clay. The trouble with this sort of approach is that no matter what soil scientists say, particle size in sand or silt can range widely; one gardener's fine sand is another's coarse silt. What you need in the greenhouse is soil that is, on the average, finer than beach sand but coarser than potter's clay. If your own garden soil is clayey, you may be able to grow great crops in it outdoors, but you should add some sand to it before using it in the greenhouse. If it's too sandy, you may be able to buy a load of good topsoil to add to it, but it's usually best to add humus, which cures all soils anyway.

HUMUS

Humus is organic matter. If soil doesn't have any humus, it's not soil, but dirt, and you can't grow anything in it (unless you're a hydroponics expert). Humus is the garden cure-all. It is possible to add too much of some things, like lime, wood ashes, or chemical fertilizer, to the garden, but it is virtually impossible to add too much humus. Dairy farmers in the Northeast have been spreading cow manure on their fields for three hundred years; it hasn't hurt the fields yet.

Humus functions in two ways to improve soil. Physically, it lightens the structure of the soil, making spaces into which roots can move and pockets that hold water (long enough but not too long) and air. This magic compound improves sandy and clayey soils alike. Many soil mixes or soil improvers, such as peat moss, that are sold in garden supply stores are mainly various kinds of humus.

Chemically, all humus contains nutrients. Some kinds are high in one element and low in another; some contain most of the elements plants need. If you apply a mix of compost and manure, and especially if you have access to more than one kind of manure, your garden soil will contain everything your plants need.

It would be difficult to find in nature dirt that didn't contain any humus, but since it's impossible to have too much humus, the gardener should use all the sources he can get his hands on. Usually these boil down to compost and manure. Composting and acquiring manures are usually outdoor activities, somewhat gross and smelly, but essential to having a successful garden.

MANURE

Common kinds of manure that most gardeners have access to include horse, cow, sheep, pig, and chicken. Less common kinds include goat, rabbit, and nowadays in some locations, bison, llama, or even more exotic creatures. Chicken and rabbit manure are much higher in most nutrients than cow or horse; sheep manure is higher in potassium than most other manures. Most of us, however, can't afford to be choosy; if we live in dairy country, we're delighted to beg a little cow manure from the farmer; if there are a lot of horses around, horse manure will do fine.

Don't make the mistake of thinking that farmers will be delighted to have you take this material off their hands. Most farmers know full well the value of this agricultural by-product. If you approach them right, however, you can probably beg an occasional pickup truck load. It doesn't hurt if you give the farmer's wife some fresh lettuce or homegrown beans from time to time. If all else fails, you can buy dried, composted sheep, cow, or other manure at the store.

A good deal has been written about the danger of using fresh manure as opposed to well rotted or composted. It is true that fresh manure applied directly to plants may burn them; powerful chemical fertilizers applied in the same way will burn them a great deal more.

Remember the old adage "Feed the soil, not the plants." Then think about what farmers do. Dairy farmers take completely fresh manure and spread it on their fields in fall. Then it lies there a few months or more before they plant corn. You should do the same thing. If you can get your hands (or at least your shovel) on a quantity of manure, grab it, particularly in early spring or fall. Store it or spread it on parts of the garden that you aren't going to use for a while. Till it in if you can. I've never had a problem with the burning of plants put in soil that had cow manure tilled into it a few weeks earlier; with chicken or rabbit manure, you might have to wait a bit longer.

In many foreign countries, human manure, often called "night soil," is used in agriculture. You probably wouldn't even consider that, but if you have a large dog or dogs, confined outdoors to a specific area, you may wonder about making use of what you have to clean up anyway. The answer is, don't. All authorities strongly discourage the use on plants of any excrement from carnivores, because it may carry parasites that could be transmitted to humans.

Manure is not a greenhouse material. You aren't going to pile a half ton of it in one corner of the greenhouse and wait for it to decompose, then spread it on your beds. What you should do is add plenty of it to your garden outside, and after a suitable interval, bring some of that soil into the greenhouse. You might occasionally put a handful of very well-aged manure in a large pot before filling it with greenhouse soil, but you would not do that very frequently.

Manure Tea

You probably won't bring any great quantity of manure into the greenhouse, but you may bring in "manure tea." Manure tea, which is the kind of term we organic gardeners love, is made very simply by "steeping" manure in water. One recipe calls for an old-fashioned bushel basket of manure suspended in a barrel of water for half a day or so. I've had good results with about that much manure tied up in a burlap bag and suspended in a trash can under the eaves. Every time the barrel fills up, I take some out and use it. Using it may be an indoor activity, but making it definitely takes place outdoors. It smells as much as you would expect. Use it in watering plants. Try not to get it on the leaves, but don't worry; it isn't very strong.

Fig. 15. Recipe for manure tea: one burlap bag of manure in one trash can of water.

COMPOST

If you are so unfortunate as to have no generous neighbors from whom you can "borrow" a ton of manure, you can still add plenty of humus to the garden in the form of compost. Even if you have access to unlimited quantities of manure, you should make compost nonetheless. In the first place, it will add substances to the garden that are missing or in short supply in manure, and in the second place, why pay the trash man to haul away materials that are valuable to you?

Some greenhousers make compost right in the greenhouse. I don't, but you can if you want to. Those who advocate it say that it is a source of heat, which of course it is, although there may be some doubt as to how much heat it provides. Composting is not terribly smelly, and it doesn't attract a great many flies and other unattractive insects, but it's not an activity I care to have going on in one room of my home. If you do compost indoors, you will probably use a manufactured composter, which resembles a large trash can with a crank for turning it over and holes for ventilation. It will smell.

If you want to compost outdoors, as most gardeners do, there are hundreds, if not thousands, of books and articles on the subject. Many make it appear that composting is as complicated and ritualistic as the Japanese tea ceremony, only it costs a lot more. I suggest a simpler approach. Build two or, better, three compost bins out of concrete blocks.

The block company in my neighborhood has a pile of seconds that are free for the asking. If you're less fortunate, you can buy them cheaply. Have the bins back up to the garden fence; in other words, make the garden fence the back side of all the bins. Have a common wall between bin one and two and between bin two and three. One standard size of block is 8 by 8 by 16. Using this size, make the bins about three blocks (48 inches) wide and three blocks long, and four or five blocks (32 to 40 inches) high. The actual dimensions can vary, but the block must be laid so that the holes show, enabling air to pass in and out. And, of course, don't cement them; just pile them up dry.

To start composting, make a pile of small branches at the bottom, not neat, but messy, to allow air circulation. Scrunched-up chicken wire will also work for this, but it's more of a nuisance when you empty the bin. Then throw all your garbage in the bin. In this case, garbage means nonanimal household wastes: coffee grounds, banana peels, tired lettuce, potato peelings, anything like that, but never any fat, meat, bones, fish, or other animal material, with one exception—eggshells, which will add valuable calcium.

Also throw in all garden waste: weeds, bean and pea vines, broccoli plants that are no longer bearing, and everything else. If you suspect that

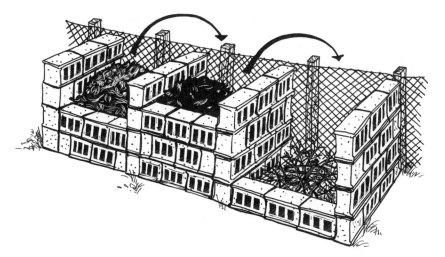

Fig. 16. A three-bin concrete block composter is functional and inexpensive.

some of your plants are seriously diseased or insect ridden, don't put them in the compost; burn them instead, if that's legal where you live. Although the heat of composting should take care of such matters, it's better to be safe. View tomato and cucurbit vines with particular suspicion.

View gifts with suspicion, also. If the town dumps grass clippings somewhere, and you can have them free for the asking, be 100 percent sure that no chemicals have been used on the lawns, which is quite unlikely. Autumn leaves in moderation are all right, but they tend to mat down. If you can let them rot for a year somewhere on your property, then use them, that's great. Some gardeners run over leaves on the lawn with the power mower again and again, shredding and piling them at once. Shredded leaves can be put in the compost without a year's aging.

Pine needles are too acid and have other drawbacks. Sawdust and wood chips are good in moderation, but they take longer to decompose than such things as celery leaves, and in the decomposition process they take nitrogen out of the surrounding material, although eventually they return it. It is often better to use them, in moderation, applied directly to the soil.

Most materials can go in just as they are, but a few have to be chopped up. Eggshells won't do you much good at all unless ground fine; a blender is excellent for this, although blending eggshells does tend to scratch the sides of the cup. Cornstalks, corncobs, the coarser stalks of broccoli, Brussels sprouts, and other brassica, as well as whole squash and pumpkins will decompose very slowly unless cut up. You can keep a short length of wooden 4x4 on the compost bin wall, hold such items with one hand, and whack them with a cleaver or hatchet. This can be risky for the fingers, and I strongly recommend that you don't do it, because I don't want to be sued. I have been told that it's not good for a brush cutter to feed soft materials into it. Do what seems right to you.

The "Japanese Tea Ceremony" school of composting will teach you just how much of this and that to add and when to turn the pile. I try to have at least as much brown stuff as green stuff, if not more. Brown, or dry, stuff is material like hay, leaves, and so forth, Green, or wet, stuff is what comes out of the kitchen or fresh material from the garden. If you let pulled weeds lie around for a week or so, they become brown. (They also drop all their seeds where they are lying, so it's not a great idea, but nobody's perfect.)

In addition to the above, add ten or twenty shovelfuls of garden soil to the pile from time to time, maybe about every two weeks, and throw some manure into it each time you get a fresh supply.

Turn over the material whenever you can get around to it, which won't be very often. Do it like this: Let's say the compost is in bin one. Put down branches or chicken wire in bin two. Turn the material from one into two, moving it over the intervening wall. A fork often works better than a shovel for this; taking the top layer of blocks off that wall as you go along also helps.

When bin one is empty, cover the material in bin two with a good layer of garden soil and leave it alone for a while. Take the sticks and branches or chicken wire out of bin one (a really messy job) and put them on the bottom of bin three. That's why having three bins works best, along with the fact that in the fall you have a lot of compostable material coming out of the garden. Put more branches on the bottom of bin one, and start a new pile there.

If you don't get around to turning the piles any oftener than I do, you may find that about halfway through the turning process, you're down to compost that's totally processed. Stop turning and start spreading it on the garden. If you have never done composting, you will be astonished at the way rotten tomatoes and other gross objects have turned into an utterly inoffensive material that looks exactly like extremely rich garden loam, which is what it is.

Worm Composting

One kind of indoor composting that is relatively inoffensive is worm composting. A worm composting bin about 2 feet by 3 feet by 14 inches can be made out of wood and plywood, with a hinged lid and about a dozen large drainage holes in the bottom. This can be kept under a shelf in the greenhouse, slightly elevated off the floor with, if desired, a sheet of plastic underneath. Bedding can be cardboard, or peat moss, but moistened shredded newspaper (no toxic dyes) works best.

A pound of red wiggler worms will consume about a half pound of garbage per day. A worm box shouldn't produce any great odor or insect problem in the greenhouse. If there are such problems, they are probably a sign that you are overfeeding the worms. One man I know feeds his worms nothing but coffee grounds. Although some authorities don't recommend it, he says it works perfectly, and of course there are no fruit flies and no aroma except that of coffee.

After a few weeks, the worms will have produced compost that is as rich and attractive as bin-produced compost, if not more so. It is harvested by shining a bright light on the top; the worms will crawl away from the light and continue to do so as you remove the compost layer by layer from the top. After the removal, start again with bedding and garbage. For more detailed information, consult your local cooperative extension office or one of the sources listed at the end of this book.

OTHER ORGANIC ADDITIVES

There are other soil additives, fertilizers, really, that don't add humus but are totally organic. These include bone meal, dried blood, fish emulsion, ground rock phosphate, seaweed, and greensand. You will learn from the labels how to use these and which nutrients they provide. Though they are not as powerful as chemical fertilizers, it is entirely possible to overuse them. Outdoors, dried blood is said to repel rabbits and deer as well as add nitrogen.

Bone meal is very high in phosphorus. It is also a desiccant, which means it attracts and absorbs moisture out of the air. Naturally, such a material is sold in paper bags. The bag soon becomes wet and tattered, and the material inside hardens like concrete. As soon as you acquire a fresh bag of bone meal, empty the contents into an empty oatmeal container. Label it at once.

Fish emulsion is more useful and easier to use in the greenhouse than most of the others. It is high in nitrogen and phosphorus but provides some potassium as well. Use it when transplanting and setting out, and at other times, sparingly, but never before the first transplant. Use it according to the directions on the label, but dilute it even more than the instructions call for. It smells, but diluted in this way it is not terribly offensive to most people and the smell fades in a few days.

SOIL SCREENING

Most natural soils contain gravel, pebbles, stones, or rocks. A New England field will astonish a midwesterner: Corn is growing, quite healthily, out of a soil littered with fist-size to head-size rocks. You may be able to grow corn outdoors in such an environment, but in the greenhouse you need soil containing few or no large particles. Screens (see chapter 2)

Fig. 17. Soil can be put through fine or coarse screening, according to your needs.

are used to get rid of them. For covering seeds, unless they are as large as peas or beans, use soil put through a kitchen strainer. For starting seedlings, use soil that has no pea-size lumps or stones. Sturdy, well-grown plants, however, will thrive in soil from which only the rocks the size of your thumb or larger have been removed. Save the gravel you acquire in this way; use it for drainage in the bottom of a pot.

CHEMICAL NATURE OF SOIL (pH)

Soils in nature (and in the garden supply store) range from very acid to very alkaline, or basic. The pH of a soil is a measure of its acidity. It has to do with hydrogen ion concentration, but that need not concern us. What we need to know is that a pH of 7 is neutral, with higher numbers being alkaline and lower acidic. We also need to know that the scale is logarithmic; soil with a pH of 6 is not just a little more acidic than soil with one of 7, but a great deal. Finally, we need to know that almost all of the plants we might want to grow in the greenhouse thrive at a range of 6.5 to 7. A few, for example camellias, like a much more acid soil. A few others, such as carnations, do best in a fairly alkaline soil.

Why does pH matter? Aside from the fact that a pH as low as 3 or as high as 9 would kill most plants instantly, small changes in pH can make it difficult or impossible for plants to absorb nutrient chemicals they need, especially trace elements like boron or calcium. This effect will be greatly ameliorated by a plentiful supply of humus in the soil. Many gardeners grow beautiful petunias or wonderful carrots in soil that does not have the perfect pH, because the soil contains large quantities of compost, manure, and other kinds of humus.

Soil Testing

A greenhouse operator, whether a hobbyist or a commercial grower, has to know the nature of his soil. You can obtain a rough idea of soil acidity by using litmus paper, which can be purchased inexpensively at most drug-stores. Follow directions that come with the paper. Generally speaking, add water to a very small quantity of soil in a test tube or similar container, shake it up, let it settle, and immerse the litmus strip in it. Red means acid, blue basic. Use care; even your fingertips can have enough acid on them to affect the outcome. The water you use has to be tested in advance and must be neutral or neutralized.

More delicate soil-testing kits can be bought from any garden supply house, and you should have one. You may also want to have your soil tested at the local cooperative extension office. Almost all states have a state agricultural college that maintains extension offices in each county. In New York, which is probably typical, pH testing is done right at the county extension office for no charge; soil samples can be sent to Cornell, the state agricultural university, for more extensive testing, which includes testing for potassium, phosphorus, nitrogen, and other nutrients, for a nominal fee. Ask the extension office for instructions before taking a soil sample; the procedure requires a certain amount of precision.

Adjusting pH

If your soil is too acid, you can easily make it more alkaline. If it is too alkaline, the procedure is somewhat more difficult. Farmers in areas like the Northeast, where the soil is naturally acid, regularly add lime, in one form or another, to their fields to make them less acid. You can do this, with caution—a little lime goes a long way. With any pH adjustment, add less than you think you need, wait several months, test again, then add more if necessary.

Wood ashes will have the same effect as lime on soil. In addition, they add potash (that's where the word *potassium* comes from) and can be obtained free for the asking in any rural area. Extension offices report a rash of soil brought in for testing that goes right off the high end of the pH scale. Gardeners new to woodburning figure that you can't put too much wood ash on the garden; they're wrong.

The usual recommendation for lowering pH is the addition of elemental sulfur. Fortunately, far more gardeners suffer from low pH than from high. Caution necessary in adding lime should be redoubled in adding sulfur, and the wait time is much longer.

The above discussion is about soil in the garden, not in the greenhouse. If you bring 5 gallons of soil into the greenhouse, then test it and try to remedy its defects, you will be dealing with amounts of lime or sulfur that are probably less than a teaspoon, a tremendous amount of mixing, and possible wait times of many months. The greenhouser should first make sure his garden soil has the correct acidity and necessary nutrients, then bring it into the greenhouse.

Note: This book assumes throughout that the reader has an outdoor garden or gardens as well as a greenhouse. For a few city readers, this may not be the case. If you have a greenhouse and no garden, you will be buying or otherwise acquiring topsoil. There is no other purchase you can make in which "let the buyer beware" is more apt. In most states, there is no legal definition of topsoil; the seller may deliver to you sand, subsoil, or construction detritus, take your money, and leave you with no recourse. Your only protection is the reputation of the seller, which you find out from talking to previous buyers, and your own careful inspection of the material before it is dumped outside your greenhouse door.

NUTRIENTS

Certain chemicals are essential to the growth of plants. The big three are nitrogen, potassium, and phosphorus, but trace elements such as calcium, boron, magnesium, sulfur, manganese, and a whole supermarket of other chemicals are also needed. The details surrounding the necessity for and interrelationship of these chemicals are extremely complex, but to simplify, nitrogen (N on the fertilizer package) is necessary for green, leafy growth; phosphorus (P) for good roots and ripening of fruit (remember, tomatoes and squash are fruit); and potassium (K) for strength and good color. Fortunately, most ordinary garden soils, especially if they have had plenty of compost and manure over the years, contain sufficient quantities of all necessary nutrients.

Commercial fertilizers will be labeled with three numbers, such as 5–10–5. This means that the material in the bag contains 5 percent (available) nitrogen, 10 percent phosphorus, and 5 percent potassium. The other 80 percent is inert material, which is necessary; a material that was anywhere near 100 percent nitrogen or phosphorus applied to a crop would destroy it.

You may feel that this book harps on organic fertilizers. It does. You can use commercial chemical fertilizers in your greenhouse (and your garden) if you want to, but no amount of 5–10–5 will produce good peppers or pretty zinnias if the soil doesn't contain enough humus, and it is very

Fig. 18. Rubbery plastic dishpans and ordinary buckets make good containers for various soil mix ingredients.

easy to overfertilize using such materials. It is just about impossible to put too much cow manure or compost on your garden, although it is possible to harm plants if the manure is too fresh.

SOIL MIXES
At your local farm or garden supply store, hardware store, supermarket, or greenhouse, you can purchase growing media, choosing from a bewildering array of products including sand, gravel, sphagnum peat moss, vermiculite, perlite, shredded bark, pulverized limestone, sulfur, and many other items. Most common are mixtures of some or all of these, with or without silt or clay. Most mixtures are called "potting soil." *Caution: Read labels carefully, especially on potting soils. Many of these are not designed for, and are bad for, starting seeds.*

Every greenhouser has his favorite mix of ingredients to make the perfect soil for his plants. Whatever works for you is fine; one mix is three parts peat moss, two parts perlite or vermiculite, one part sand, and five parts good garden soil. If the garden soil is lacking in humus (in which case it isn't good garden soil), use three parts soil and two parts humus (compost, manure, or both) to make up the five parts. For starting seeds, use more sand, peat, and perlite and less of the other ingredients, unless you have a problem with damping-off or other diseases, in which case you may want to start seeds in commercial seed starter only. For most herbs, increase the percentage of sand. For cacti and succulents, use almost pure sand and coarse gravel, with only a bit of soil and humus.

By now, you may be ready to give up. Nitrogen, humus, manganese, pH—how can you possibly supply all the ingredients in the proper proportion while making sure no disease has crept in? Cheer up! Remember that seeds have been germinating for millenia without your help. Seeds contain within themselves all the ingredients they need to germinate and thrive. It is only later on, after the first true leaves appear, that they need any outside nourishment (apart from water, of course), and even then they don't need much. Good garden soil, especially if modified by your addition of humus and lightening ingredients like vermiculite, contains everything your plants need.

Most plants that die indoors (and quite a few that die outdoors) die from too much care on the part of the gardener: too much water, too much fertilizer, or both. Give them moderate water, a very few nutrients, all the light possible, warmth but not too much, and all the love and attention possible, and they will thrive. If you can't or don't, they may very well thrive anyway.

Air and Water

Plants need air and water, just as animals do. In the case of plants, the two needs are very much intertwined. Too much water, or water in the wrong place, can interfere severely with the respiration of plants.

PLANT RESPIRATION

Plants breathe, but their breathing is somewhat more complicated than that of animals. Usually, to simplify, we say that animals breathe in oxygen and breathe out carbon dioxide, whereas plants breathe in carbon dioxide and breathe out oxygen. Some authorities have speculated that that's why houseplants thrive when their owners talk to them: The one-way conversation provides a carbon dioxide–rich atmosphere. Certainly that is why science-fiction spaceships, and some real ones, have plants aboard: The plants convert the CO_2 breathed out by the astronauts to oxygen.

The true situation is more complicated. Plants take in CO_2 and give off oxygen only when they have a considerable amount of light; at night they do just the reverse, giving off carbon dioxide and absorbing oxygen. Overall, however, they are net consumers of CO_2 and producers of oxygen.

Plants will thrive in an atmosphere much richer in CO_2 than humans would enjoy. Other than talking to your plants, there isn't much you can do to put more CO_2 into the greenhouse, unless you want to do what some commercial growers in the Netherlands do: buy cylinders of carbon dioxide and release the contents very slowly. The fact that they find this cost-effective is an indication of how much better plants produce under these conditions.

There is another thing that might help a little: Decomposing organic material, like manure or compost, gives off carbon dioxide. You probably don't want a large manure pile in your greenhouse, but a mulch of dried manure, compost, straw, peat moss, sawdust—any or all of these—will make a slight but useful addition to the carbon dioxide content of the greenhouse atmosphere. The decaying mulch will also provide a slight but still helpful increase in temperature. A mulch like this on the soil right around the plants, as opposed to a pile of compost in a corner, will provide the warmth and carbon dioxide at exactly the point at which it is needed.

VENTILATION AND AIR QUALITY

A greenhouse must be thoroughly ventilated. For a full discussion of ventilation, see *Building Your Own Greenhouse*, the previous book in the Greenhouse Basics series. Suffice it to say here that a greenhouse needs a well-designed ventilation system that will permit a complete change of air every few hours without chilling any of the plants, even those nearest the vents or fans.

With an attached greenhouse, ventilation from within the house is possible and desirable. What is stale air to a human is air rich in carbon dioxide to a plant, and the oxygen given off by the inhabitants of the greenhouse might as well be ventilated into the house for the benefit of the denizens thereof.

There is one kind of air that seems stale to a human that seems even more stale—in fact, poisonous—to a plant: polluted air. Among the thousands of reasons not to smoke, add this one: If you are a gardener and you smoke, you are not only poisoning yourself and the rest of your family, but you are poisoning your beloved plants as well. If someone in your household smokes, don't let

Fig. 19. A louvered exhaust fan should be high in the greenhouse wall. Some greenhousers prefer intake fans; others like exhaust fans. In either case, there must be a louvered vent in the opposite wall.

him or the gases he exudes near your plants. Aside from the fumes, the touch of someone with tobacco on his hands can spread tobacco mosaic virus.

Many other kinds of fumes also can cause death or stunted growth in plants. Wood, gas, or oil heaters can give off fumes that are deleterious to plants, and other sources of air pollution can arise in a house and influence an attached green-house. Probably the best way to provide your plants with good-quality air at the proper tem-perature is to run it through your house, and possibly your lungs, first. Remember, if you don't like the air quality in your house, you can leave; plants can't.

Fig. 20. "No smoking" must always be the rule in the greenhouse.

Given the limited space in the greenhouse, it is tempting to crowd plants. Don't do it. It is surprising how often gardeners think a plant is suffering from insects, disease, or poor nutrition, when all it really needs is more space to allow the full circulation of air around all its parts. Further-more, crowded plants are more likely to suffer from insects and disease.

THE WATERING CYCLE

Many gardeners do not realize that even the roots of plants need air. When a plant "drowns" because the soil it is in is saturated with water, it drowns for the same reason an animal does—because it is deprived of air. To the greenhouser, this means several things. First, soil must not be a heavily compacted material, like clay, but must have some coarser parti-cles that allow drainage. A certain amount of sand or fine gravel is useful for this; humus is even more useful, since it allows drainage but keeps soil from drying out too quickly.

A second factor has to do with the watering cycle. Indoors or out, it is far better if the soil gets a thorough soaking and then is allowed to dry out completely than if it gets a sketchy watering every day or two. Many seedlings, such as tomatoes, may even wilt slightly between waterings with no ill effects. If one of them does not revive when watered, it was proba-bly weak and would not have done well anyway. The others will be stronger and healthier when they reach maturity.

The tinier the plant and the smaller the amount of soil available to it, the more quickly it can die from lack of water. The small-cell flats recommended in this book have this drawback: They will need much more frequent watering. In the worst-case scenario, if they are in hot direct sunlight for a long period each day, they may need twice-a-day waterings, especially when the seedlings first begin to emerge.

To add to all your other watering concerns, some plants need much more frequent watering than others. Of course, cacti and succulents need infrequent waterings, but you will find from experience that cabbages, tomatoes, petunias, and cosmos all use water at different rates. You just have to watch them. A common problem, especially when plants get larger, is that the ones nearest the greenhouse glazing, which receive more sunlight than the others, will wilt and need water sooner.

Some experts say that some plants may never show any sign of needing water in the greenhouse, but will do poorly much later in the garden because they were deprived of water earlier. For example, seed catalogs say that if baby celeries get too dry, they will bolt (go to seed) months later. I can't personally vouch for this. Some of my celery plants have wilted totally in the greenhouse; none has ever gone to seed. I stick to my belief that far more plants are killed by overwatering than by underwatering. Eternal vigilance is the price of good greenhouse plants.

Bottom Watering

The most important rule for watering is this: All plants in the greenhouse, with the exception of cacti and succulents, should always be bottom watered; that is, they should be watered by placing the whole flat or pot containing the plants in water of a suitable depth. Cacti and succulents should be potted in a gravelly, sandy mixture that drains rapidly. They should be watered from the top infrequently but thoroughly, then allowed to drain immediately. They should never stand in water.

Bottom watering is not as difficult as it sounds. In fact, it's easier than sprinkling, unless the greenhouse boasts an automatic sprinkling system. The greenhouse must have an ample supply of water containers, especially trays of all kinds, shallow and deep. If your greenhouse has these and an ample supply of good-quality water, watering is easy. Immerse the flats and pots in water that is deep in relation to the flat or pot, but not so deep that the water rises above the top. Go away and come back in a while. You will easily be able to tell if the water, by capillary action, has reached the top of the plant container. It will be darker and shiny in appearance, and damp but not wet to the touch. If this is the case, remove the watered containers and place them on another tray to drain. It does no harm to most plants if they remain in water for an hour or so longer than necessary, but there are exceptions. Even immersion overnight won't hurt most good-sized plants, although it may be injurious to seedlings.

WATER TEMPERATURE

After bottom watering, the second most important rule for watering is this: Warm the water. If you have your own well, water probably comes into the house year-round at a temperature in the 50s. If you use city water, the temperature may be warmer than that in the summer but colder in the winter and early spring, when you will do most greenhouse watering. Cold water can stress plants, especially tiny seedlings, terribly. Ideally, water should be the temperature of the soil the plants are in. If you are finding it difficult to keep your greenhouse warm enough, even water a bit warmer than the soil (but definitely not hot) can be useful. The ideal water temperature for most plants is 65 to 75 degrees. If it is possible to water different plants at different temperatures, cool-weather crops like cabbages and their cousins prefer cooler water; peppers and eggplants wouldn't mind if the water was 80 degrees.

Don't neglect this requirement. Heat water in a kettle and mix it with cold water, use warm water from the bathtub, or let the water stand in the

Fig. 21. Bottom water your flats in tepid water.

greenhouse until it is tepid, but *don't* shock your plants with an icy bath. Some luxuriously appointed greenhouses have hot and cold water laid on, which helps with water temperature but may pose a problem with water quality.

Water Quality

Water pollution in the greenhouse is even more common than air pollution, because water that is not polluted from the human point of view may be poisonous to plants. If you have city water, it probably is chlorinated, and it may well contain far too much chlorine for the health of your plants. Fluoridation can also harm plants. In both cases, a small amount of the chemical won't be harmful. Your city water department may be able to tell you about the degree of chlorination or fluoridation, but a better source of information on this subject is a commercial greenhouse owner in your city.

One solution to this problem is to find another source of water for the greenhouse, such as rainwater or snowmelt. A more common solution for chlorinated water is to draw water from the tap and allow it to stand for several days. Usually enough chlorine will dissipate to make the water safe. Home aquarium owners deal with the problem in the same way.

If you have your own water supply in the country, from a spring, pond, or well, you are probably much better off than your city cousin. If your water is hard, it is probably very good for your plants. There are exceptions, depending on which chemical salts the water contains. You may have to have your water analyzed or discuss the problem with the county agent.

A common ingredient of hard water is calcium, and a common technique for water softening is the substitution of sodium salts for calcium salts. Unfortunately, the softened water is not as good for plants as the hard water, but there's a neat, simple, and permanent solution. Have a plumber (or do it yourself—it's not that hard) tap into the water supply before it enters the softener, and run a line from there to the greenhouse. This will give you a handy supply of hard water that will benefit your plants. Furthermore, although softened water may be better for your dishwasher, it's worse for you to drink, so you can keep a jug of greenhouse water in the refrigerator for human consumption.

Graywater

Graywater is household wastewater that does not contain human waste. In other words, it's the water that flows out of your shower, bathtub, sinks, dishwasher, and washing machine. Laws regarding graywater vary from state to state and municipality to municipality, but it's almost impossible to imagine a situation in which disease could be transmitted by the application of bathwater to a garden. Common sense suggests washing vegetables before eating them. The hypercareful might limit the use of such water to plants that are not eaten. Water containing bleach should be diluted a great deal before it is used on plants.

Though graywater is more likely to be used in the garden than in the greenhouse, it would do no harm to occasionally scoop water from the dishpan or bathtub and use it on greenhouse plants, both because this conserves water and because graywater contains small quantities of useful nutrients. If you find that your greenhouse begins to smell like an NFL locker room, you can eliminate or cut back on the practice.

Heat and Light

In the greenhouse, both heat and light come primarily from the sun. This is particularly true of the hobby greenhouse. A commercial rose grower may have to spend thousands of dollars a week on oil heat in January to get his product ready for the all-important Valentine's Day season, but most of us greenhousers derive 90 percent or more of the light and heat used for growing our plants from the sun.

SOLAR HEAT

Your greenhouse should be well designed to maximize the production of solar heat within the building and minimize heat loss at night or on cloudy days. For a discussion of glazing materials, placement of glazed areas, insulation, and caulking, see *Greenhouse Basics: Building Your Own Greenhouse.*

Preventing Overheating

Heat in a greenhouse is similar to water in this regard: It is more likely that plants will be injured by too much of it than by too little. Any greenhouse, but in particular one that has roof as well as wall glazing, can overheat in the spring and summer months, from April to September. Unless precautions are taken, it is not unusual for temperatures inside such a building to rise to well above 120 degrees, which is hot enough to kill some plants and injure others severely.

There are two ways to prevent overheating. One is to reduce the amount of glazed area; the other, more common, practice is through ventilation. In earlier times, the standard method of reducing the glazed area for a commercial greenhouse, one that is still in use to some extent, was whitewashing. In late spring or early summer, a white compound was sprayed on the exterior of the glass. This material was so designed that a succession of summer rains washed it off; ideally, enough of it was gone by October that it did not need to be removed manually.

Whitewash doesn't work well on glazing materials other than glass, and most hobby greenhouse owners, even those who use glass, don't trouble with it. Instead, they, like the majority of commercial greenhouse owners, cover the top glazed surfaces with shade cloth. This is reasonably inexpensive and lasts several seasons. It is not difficult to apply on freestanding greenhouses, although it may be a pain to work with on attached greenhouses that have a few skylights or an entire glass roof. Some arrangement with inexpensive plastic tarpaulins may have to be worked out for such structures.

A shutter or curtain arrangement *inside* the greenhouse, though it may be much more convenient, will do just about nothing to cut down on overheating. Such an arrangement may help slightly to prevent loss of heat on winter nights, but it won't keep plants cool in the summer.

Most hobby gardeners who have freestanding greenhouses either don't use them during the summer months or cool them with ventilation. This may also be necessary with an attached greenhouse, although one with an opaque roof and extensive roof overhangs functions like a solar house and is seldom hotter in summer than the house to which it is attached, although it will be in spring, fall, and winter. In contrast, it takes a great deal of ventilation to keep a glass-roofed greenhouse even moderately cool in the summertime. Either there must be screened, openable doors and windows on more than one side of the building, or there must be vents, in which case fans must be kept going most of the time.

In April and May, there will be days when it is far too cold outdoors for plants but far too warm inside the greenhouse. Care must be taken on these days so that cold air entering the greenhouse is warmed somewhat before it strikes tender plants. Commercial greenhouses have complicated heat exchangers, basically perforated pipes that carry the incoming air around inside the building, allowing it to be warmed before too much of it escapes. The hobby greenhouser who doesn't want to incur that much expense just has to do the best he can. Generally, if the intake vent is near the floor and the exhaust is up high, and tender plants are kept off the floor, there will not be too much problem.

This is when the attached greenhouse that is designed to function as a solar heating device, as well as a room in which to grow plants, comes into its own. If it is well designed, it will have one or two large doors that lead into the main house, as well as two or more vents high up on the common wall between the house and the greenhouse. The greenhouser can fine-tune the degree to which each of these is open, warming the house and cooling the greenhouse in the daytime, and warming the greenhouse while cooling the house, if desired, at night.

HEATING IN WINTER

After working all summer to keep the greenhouse cool, the poor greenhouser must work all winter to keep it warm. Rarely will the sun alone suffice. Some artificial heat is necessary, not so much on the coldest days as on the cloudiest ones, and of course at night.

A well-designed attached greenhouse with sufficient insulation and heat-sink material will not need much supplemental heat. If, in addition, there is a system of shutters to cover the glazed area at night, it will need very little. But it will still need some. This supplemental heat can probably be obtained from the house, either through openings or simply by leakage through the wall and glass doors. (It is not only unnecessary but also unwise to insulate the wall between the greenhouse and the house.)

Whether additional heat will be needed depends not only on the construction of the greenhouse, but also on what use you make of it in the coldest, darkest months. If nothing is grown, or if only cold-hardy plants like lettuce and radishes are cultivated, less heat will be needed than if tomatoes or African violets are being grown.

If the plants need more warmth than can be obtained by simply allowing heat from the house to flow into the greenhouse, or if the design makes that impossible, then some nonsolar heat source is necessary. Most artificial heat comes from combustion—that is, from burning fuels like coal, wood, or gas. Combustion gives off gases, many of which are harmful to plants as well as to people.

Almost any source of combustion located in the greenhouse will give off fumes. There are greenhousers who use kerosene heaters or wood stoves and swear that they do the plants no harm, but most gardeners with considerable experience in this area are certain that such people are deluding themselves. A plant may look quite healthy to its loving owner but literally pale by comparison with another from a better environment. Having a wood stove in the greenhouse, although it is done, is one of the least practical and desirable ways to provide supplemental heat. Although, theoretically, "airtight" stoves shouldn't give off any fumes, in practice most wood stoves smoke or release gases, even if it's only when the door is opened. Most wood stoves are difficult to adjust, giving off too little heat one moment and too much the next.

Fig. 22. Unfortunately, plants can't let you know when fumes are choking them.

Electric Heat

The best heating arrangement for a greenhouse involves having the combustion take place elsewhere. Basically, this is what electric heat does, the combustion usually taking place hundreds of miles away or not at all, as when the electricity is generated by water power or nuclear fission. The best heat for a greenhouse or any other building is electric heat, except for one small problem: In most parts of the United States and Canada, it costs much more per unit of heat than burning wood, gas, oil, or coal.

If you need only a small amount of artificial heat for your greenhouse, then it is certainly best to use electricity, in one of three ways. The first, most extensive, and most expensive method is to install one or more electric baseboard heaters. The fact that your greenhouse probably doesn't have baseboards needn't deter you; baseboard heaters don't require baseboards. Such heaters are relatively inexpensive and easy to install. You can do it yourself if you're handy and the local building code permits.

The second method is a small, self-contained radiator. The smallest of these are on wheels so that they may be placed where the need is greatest. They sometimes are filled with water, but more often with oil, which has certain advantages, one being that it won't freeze and burst the radiator as readily as water. They can be plugged into any outlet and include a ther-

Fig. 23. A small, portable electric radiator is one of the best ways to provide supplementary heating in the greenhouse.

mostat, so that they can be set to turn themselves on and off at the greenhouser's discretion. These are extremely popular with small hobby greenhousers.

The third method is the most common and is often used in conjunction with other heat sources. It is a soil or flat heater. In most cases, particularly with sprouting seeds, it is not the air temperature, but the soil temperature, that is crucial. Most garden supply houses stock several kinds of these heaters, and many seed catalogs offer them.

Soil heaters come in a variety of sizes and prices, but two kinds are most common. One consists simply of insulated wire; the other is a mat or grid. Each has a built-in thermostat. Neither is terribly expensive, but the mat costs more than the wire. I recommend the mat type. My experience may be unique, but after a couple of years' use and no abuse, a wire-type heater short-circuited and started to fill my greenhouse with smoke. Fortunately, I was at home and nearby when it happened. A much more common experience is to have a thermostat fail and all the plants in the greenhouse freeze or bake. There is a certain risk involved in leaving a greenhouse unattended for any length of time and relying on mechanical devices.

Fig. 24. A mat heater is preferable to a wire coil for heating flats.

Other Sources of Heat

If your home has oil or gas heat, another way to have the combustion take place outside the greenhouse is to have the hot air, hot water, or steam circulate through radiators, baseboard heaters, or registers in the greenhouse. Usually such an arrangement is made when the house and greenhouse are built, but a competent plumbing and heating expert can add certain kinds of units in the greenhouse after the fact.

A relatively new device is the outdoor wood furnace. In rural areas, you will see these outside of farmhouses. They look like giant Log Cabin syrup cans; if you aren't familiar with those, they look like quite small houses, complete with chimney, made of metal.

The outdoor wood furnace is such a simple idea that it's remarkable no one thought of it sooner. It consists of a furnace that burns wood, surrounded by a boiler, all very well insulated. It is usually about 100 feet from the house. Pipes buried underground conduct hot water to the house, where it circulates through radiators or baseboard heaters then, cooled, returns to the boiler. All the fuss, mess, and danger of wood heating is outdoors. There is a major drawback to all this for the greenhouser, however: Even the smallest unit, designed to heat a four-room house, would be a bit pricey to install just for a greenhouse, but it is at least something to think about if you live in the country and have access to a plentiful supply of wood.

LIGHT

There is one important way in which light differs from heat: It is impossible to have too much of it, at least at most U.S. latitudes and for the greenhouse as a whole, or for most of the plants you might grow in it, although there are some plants that do better in partial or complete shade. Obtaining maximum light means not only using all the glazing possible, but also painting surfaces white to reflect more light.

As with most things in life, however, there are trade-offs. There are drawbacks to having too much glazing in an attached greenhouse, particularly in the roof, and heat-sink areas should not be light colored, but as dark as possible, in order to absorb energy for later release. Material like slate or brick is usually dark colored, and concrete knee walls might be painted black, whereas walls of Sheetrock or a similar material could be white or a light pastel color.

It is important to realize that some plants, especially those usually regarded as houseplants, do not thrive in too much direct sunlight. Attached greenhouses, especially those with minimal roof glazing, have areas, usually on the north side, that are ideal for plants that prefer little or no direct sunlight. In other greenhouses, it may be necessary to keep such plants under benches or shelves, at least part of the time.

Countering Phototropism

Plants that have too little light become leggy as they stretch upward toward the sun or other light source. Most plants are also phototropic, which means that they lean toward the light source. They are particularly prone to do this when it is cloudy. If the only sunlight in your greenhouse comes from glazing in walls, it may be necessary during the months when the sun is low in the sky, from about September to March, to turn flats and movable beds to counteract this tendency. It may even be necessary, or at least desirable, to place some flats under west windows in the afternoon and carry them across to east windows when the sun sets.

This may sound like a lot of work, but it is necessary primarily with small seedlings, which is one argument for not starting seeds in immovable beds, but transplanting into such beds when the plants have achieved some size. Mature plants in pots may benefit from being turned once a week or so. If you move pots to bottom water them, you can make a note of which side of the pot was toward the sun, or you can figure that the law of averages will result in the plant not always having the same side toward the sun.

Artificial Light

For most plants, solar light, like solar heat, must be supplemented to some degree or other in the dark months. There aren't as many variations on artificial light as there are on heat, nor do we need to light the entire greenhouse area. Commercial growers may keep the entire greenhouse ablaze with light on December evenings, but it's unlikely that you or I would want to pay the cost of such total lighting. Most of us will make do with a few fluorescent tubes over plants that particularly need help getting started in the dark months. Incandescent bulbs (the pear-shaped ones) are nearly useless in providing light for plants, although they can be used as supplemental heaters in a small area. Greenhousers use fluorescents that are usually called "grow-lights" or have a similar trade name, such as Gro-lite. Ordinary cool-white or warm-white tubes or, better yet, a combination of the two function nearly as well as grow-lights, but the latter are now so inexpensive that they might as well be used. A few years ago they were about $20 each; the last ones I bought cost $7.

The usual and best arrangement makes use of one or more inexpensive 4-foot shop brackets that hold two 40-watt tubes. Each bracket is suspended with lightweight chains that come with it. The chief thing to

Fig. 25. These fluorescent growing lights could be even closer to the seedlings.

remember about grow-lights is that they should be as close to the plants as possible. Suspend them a few inches above the tops of the plants, and move them up as the plants grow.

Gardeners, like other human beings, often suffer from the delusion that if a little of something is good, a lot of it will be better. Practice moderation in all things. Specifically, don't leave the artificial light on the plants all night long, or even most of the night. Plants need a dark period to complete the photosynthesis process begun in the light. Fourteen hours is about the maximum amount of total light—whether natural, artificial, or both—that your plants should receive.

Now comes a heretical idea: Sometimes you don't even need a greenhouse, just a couple of grow-lights in a warm basement in January. If you're going to start seeds in the darkest months, you will almost certainly need artificial light and heat, unless you live quite far south.

Pests and Diseases

With regard to insects and diseases in the greenhouse, an ounce of prevention isn't worth a pound of cure. It's worth more like a ton. To protect your precious plants from contamination, you will need to take what may seem to be extreme measures.

BRINGING IN PLANTS

If someone gives you a plant to add to your collection, place it in quarantine for at least a month. Do the same thing with plants dug up outdoors in fall to be brought indoors. The best quarantine location is a deck or porch outside, near the greenhouse but not too near, and somewhat protected from cold and wind. It is not difficult to make sure that plants you dig up in your garden stay in quarantine a month; just dig them up a month before the expected first frost date. If it isn't convenient to dig them up until later, put them on the deck and move them into a slightly more protected spot, like a shed or garage, *not* the greenhouse, when frost is threatened. Move them back the next day.

This would be a good practice even if there were no fear of insects or disease. Call it softening up, the opposite of hardening off. Plants can profit from an intermediate step between the bright sun and cool nights of the fall garden and the darker, warmer conditions of the greenhouse. No greenhouse is ever as bright as outdoors.

You may have to be rude with people to protect your plants; believe me, it's a necessary evil. Friends and acquaintances of greenhousers often "lend" plants to be kept over the cold months or indefinitely. Your attitude toward this ought to be no different from your attitude if they asked you to keep a wayward puppy or difficult child for an indefinite period: They'd have to be awfully good friends.

Most plants aren't wayward, although some may seem to be, but some are difficult, and many are infested with aphids or infected with fungi. Your best bet is to let your friends think you are inept or eccentric. If you have no other example of the plant in your collection, say, "Oh, I never have any luck with begonias; I'd surely kill it." Then stick to your guns.

If he insists beyond all measure, take his plant. Don't put it in the greenhouse; kill it. That's what you said would happen, isn't it? If you have fifty geraniums and he wants to have you keep his also, say, "OK, but I'll have to leave it out in quarantine for a month, and the nights are quite cold now." If he insists, do just that.

While plants are in quarantine, water them very sparingly and inspect them regularly. Use a magnifying glass. If one seems to be diseased or insect-ridden, *throw it out!* Not in the compost, either. Burn it, bury it deep, not in the garden, or take it a long way from home and throw it in the woods. Don't worry about infecting the woods; there will be plenty of creatures there to cope with the aphids or bacteria. And *don't* save the pot, although if it's a really beautiful china specimen, you might make an exception and wash it thoroughly in warm, soapy water, rinse it, and then let it stand in a mild bleach solution for an hour.

Finally, before bringing new acquisitions into the greenhouse, it's a good idea to bare-root them. Knock them out of the pot, wash the roots thoroughly, using a fairly strong stream from the hose, and inspect the roots as well as the stems, leaves, and blossoms, if any, with the magnifying glass. If the plant passes inspection, bring it in and repot it in the clean pots and safe soil you keep in the greenhouse.

Plants from your own or someone else's garden are less risky than someone else's house or greenhouse plants, including those from the florist. In the garden, plants grow strong and resistant or they die, and whiteflies and diseases have a host of natural enemies. In the artificial environment of the greenhouse, things are different; you've possibly heard a weak, delicate person described as a "hothouse flower."

Greenhousers whose birthdays or anniversaries are in May or June have healthier plants than those born in December. Can you figure that out? When people give them gift plants, they can keep them on the dining table for a couple of weeks, then stick them in the garden. Either they'll die or they'll probably be safe to bring in by fall. Either way, not much is lost. Florists' plants are often forced to bloom at sale time. After the forced bloom period, they won't do much for a long time anyway.

DEALING WITH INFESTATION OR DISEASE

I used to grow impatiens. They always became infested with red spider mites. I stopped trying to grow impatiens; the problem disappeared. When I find a plant infested with aphids, often a tiny basil, I put it out in the snow and leave it there. The basil dies, and so do the aphids. Occasionally it is possible, with a hardy plant, to freeze the insects and not the plant. Or heat may do it; some say that you can immerse a plant in water that is about 200 degrees for half an hour or so and sometimes save the plant but kill the insects or bacteria. It hardly seems worth it to me.

You may detect what seems to be a callous attitude in the above paragraphs. Soft-hearted people make lousy gardeners. Weeding out unwanted or infected plants is called *roguing,* and a good gardener will rogue out weaklings without mercy. Plants are not children; you can always grow another one.

AVOIDING DISEASE TRANSFER

Above all, don't pet a sick plant or examine it with your fingers; you'll just pass the disease on. Wash your hands as frequently as an operating room surgeon. Insist that visitors behave as you do. Most assuredly, don't let them smoke in the greenhouse. Even if they aren't smoking at the moment, don't let smokers into the greenhouse if you can possibly avoid it; they could give some of your plants tobacco mosaic virus.

A standard remedy for an infested greenhouse is a "bomb," which releases a poisonous gas to fumigate the premises. When you clean your greenhouse annually, you could conclude with this, closing and hermetically sealing all doors, windows, vents, and cracks. This might kill all the aphids and spider mites; it would almost surely kill all the ladybugs and spiders, and could seep into the house and kill your cat or make him sick.

The fundamental thing to understand about insect pests and diseases is that you can control them, but you can never eradicate them. There will always be aphids in the garden and probably in the greenhouse. It is only when they become too numerous that you have to take action.

Both insects and disease are much more serious problems on plants that are born, live, and die without ever going outdoors. If you start seedlings in the greenhouse and transplant them into the garden, and if you put your houseplants (those for which this is suitable) in the garden in summer, you will have fewer and less serious problems.

CLEANLINESS AND HYGIENE

Use clean pots and throw out, into the garden or compost, all growth media that was not purchased, such as sand or garden soil or mixtures containing these, at the end of the greenhouse season. For most, that will be about July 1, when all the plants can be safely put into the garden. Clean the entire greenhouse thoroughly at that time. Don't disinfect it; just sweep, throw out all the stuff that has accumulated, and wash the floor and all other surfaces with soap and water.

If your greenhousing is a continuous operation, try to find some date on which you can perform the above tasks. Perhaps you can take a few dozen plants from the greenhouse into the house in order to effect this. Bring in new soil as late as you can, preferably after a few hard freezes. I find that I can often dig soil from south-facing slopes during a January thaw; I don't need much soil before then anyway.

SOIL STERILIZATION

Many books give directions for the sterilization of soil, often suggested to prevent diseases, especially damping-off. The two methods usually recommended are baking in the kitchen range or drenching with a very dilute solution of a bleach, such as Clorox. Heating soil in the stove is awkward, messy, and smelly. Treating it with bleach is tricky, and if you use such a chemical, you can't really claim to be an organic gardener, if that matters to you. Either practice kills just about all the beneficial organisms in the soil, thus changing it to plain old dirt. I don't recommend these practices, but if you wish to try them, one method is to heat soil to 180 degrees for thirty minutes. This is accomplished by putting a quantity of soil in the stove with a thermometer stuck in it and turning off the heat when the thermometer reaches 180.

Without soil sterilization, the other hygienic practices outlined above will protect you from about 99 percent of the "bad bugs," be they insects, fungi, viruses, or bacteria, that might attack your plants. The practices may seem extreme, but I can tell you this: In over ten years with my present greenhouse, I've never had any serious problem with insects or disease, and I've had very few minor ones.

"GOOD BUGS"

The "bad bug" populations in my greenhouse are kept under control by the "good bug" populations. "Good bugs" may not be a very scientific term, but it's convenient shorthand for viruses, bacteria, nematodes, insects, and other creatures that destroy the creatures that hurt plants.

Fig. 26. An adult ladybug.

In the garden, one of the best "good bugs" is a toad. There are drawbacks to keeping toads and snakes in the greenhouse, but you can keep plenty of other predators there, most of which you'll never see. Most people have heard about the work of ladybugs and mantises. Mantises are overrated; they eat each other and do little to discourage tiny creatures like aphids. Ladybugs, especially the larvae, are voracious consumers of aphids and other baddies, but they have a bad habit of wandering off your premises. I don't buy them anymore, although when I find one wintering over in the house— a common occurrence— I catch it and release it in the greenhouse.

Fig. 27. This rather unattractive creature, a ladybug larva, eats its weight in aphids in a very short time.

Trichogramma wasps and other varieties, all of them tiny, are parasitic predators on many pests, most of them caterpillars. Caterpillars are not too common in the greenhouse, but if you are troubled by them, you can buy these wasps, in the form of eggs or larvae, from specialty suppliers (see the Appendix).

Green lacewings, both adults and larvae, prey on aphids and many other greenhouse pests. They are available from the same sources as wasps.

Fig. 28. This wasp in reality is about the size of a fennel seed, but it is a useful predator.

Fig. 29. A lacewing like this one preys on insect pests, as does its larva.

My greenhouse is full of spiders, and I do nothing to discourage them; in fact, I try to avoid killing one. As far as I know, nobody sells spiders, probably because most people don't find them cute, but they are carnivorous (although some arachnids, like mites, are not), and the ones in my greenhouse must be eating something. I suspect it's something I want eaten.

Fig. 30. Spiders like this house spider are the most maligned of creatures. They rarely hurt humans but will control many greenhouse pests.

There are probably hundreds of "good bugs" in the greenhouse—in the soil, on the plants, in the air, in the water, and in the cracks and crevices. They'll do a great deal for you and expect nothing in return, except the occasional square meal, if you don't kill them in a misguided attempt to destroy what they feed on.

If you see an insect in the greenhouse and you don't know it to be harmful, let it alone. The odds are very high that it is beneficial (from your point of view) or that, like a dung beetle, it does you neither good nor harm. There is one rough rule of thumb: If it is easy to catch and kill, it is probably something harmful or neutral. Predator bugs usually scramble out of your clutches faster than herbivores.

OTHER ORGANIC INSECT CONTROLS

Solutions to insect problems include insect predators or other predators like you. When you put beer out for slugs, squish aphids with your fingers, or discard an infested plant, you are functioning as a predator. If no other solution works, you can spray. Sometimes simply a strong spray of clear water will wash insects off plants; many bugs are too fragile to survive this.

Showers

Some very successful indoor gardeners give most of their potted plants (not cacti and similar kinds) a weekly shower. They put the pot in the bathtub and turn on tepid water from overhead. This gets rid of many insects before the gardener has even begun to notice them, and the "rain" is good for most plants.

Other Sprays

The next step is a soap spray. You can buy an insecticidal soap solution, or you can put a drop of dishwashing liquid in a gallon of water. Other popular organic sprays involve garlic, onion, hot pepper, or a combination thereof, ground up and mixed with a great deal of water. A certified organic farmer I know makes "nettle tea" by leaving nettles in water in a barrel outdoors "until it stinks to high heaven," then diluting the tea ten to one or more. He recommends it highly; it may smell up your greenhouse, but it will kill many bugs.

Bt

Bt stands for *Bacillus thuringiensis.* There are many different Bt's, for mosquitoes, blackflies, leaf-eating caterpillars, and other undesirable insects. All are totally organic and totally safe, since they are in essence diseases that caterpillars, for instance, can catch and you and your dog can't. They won't hurt any insect except the one, or the type, for which they are specific. You probably aren't troubled by mosquitoes or caterpillars in your greenhouse, but if fungus gnats are a nuisance to you, there is a Bt for them.

Other Organic Poisons

A few years back, rotenone and pyrethrum, or pyrethrins, were all the rage with organic gardeners, including me. Now I never use them. They are organic in the sense that they are made from plants; rotenone is made from the root of a South American plant, and pyrethrum from a variety of chrysanthemum. Unfortunately, both can kill creatures you don't want killed, like spiders and ladybugs, or, in the garden, bees. Rotenone is particularly deadly to fish. You may not keep fish in the greenhouse, although a few greenhousers do, but pesticides have a way of getting into the water table.

Traps

Insect traps are not usually used in the greenhouse, except for one kind. Aphids, whiteflies, and many other undesirables are attracted to bright yellow. You can buy sticky 3-by-5-inch "cards" of this color, or circles of the same material, and set them up as traps. Hundreds of bugs will get stuck on them; when one gets too gross, throw it away and set up another one in the wire holder that comes with it. If you are really thrifty, you can buy a bottle of the sticky stuff, clean dirty traps with cooking oil, and recoat them.

CHEMICAL PESTICIDES AND FUNGICIDES

If you want to use powerful chemicals in your greenhouse, go to the garden supply store, buy something on the shelf, and follow the directions on the label. For example, some authorities recommend drenching soil with Diazinon to get rid of root mealybugs. I would rather have a lot of bugs in my greenhouse or throw out some plants than use a product that the law forbids golf courses or turf farms to use. (The windrows of dead geese upset the golfers, anyway.)

If you must buy and use powerful chemical insecticides, at least don't be the kind of idiot who figures that if one teaspoonful is good, three must be better. The company wants you to use up the product as soon as possible; they're not going to tell you to use too little. Try using half as much. That's a good rule with organic sprays and all kinds of fertilizers as well.

For some odd reason, some gardeners who wouldn't dream of using malathion or Diazinon to get rid of insects regularly spray with sulfur or copper compounds or even lead arsenate to get rid of diseases, most of which are fungi. They appear to believe that it's all right to use chemicals to kill disease. Unfortunately, some fungicides, like many herbicides, will harm bees or your dog or even you.

This odd behavior on the part of supposedly "organic" gardeners may stem from the fact that, unfortunately, there are few good organic controls for disease after it appears in your greenhouse. Prevention involves disease-free or disease-resistant seeds and plants and the hygienic practices described previously.

SOME SPECIFIC INSECTS

Aphids

Aphids are probably the most common greenhouse pest. These tiny, soft-bodied insects suck juices out of stems or leaves of plants. They are often green, but can be off-white, black, or almost any other color. Curling leaves may be a sign of them; they can usually

Fig. 31. The aphid is probably the worst pest in the greenhouse.

be seen by very close inspection. If stems look bumpy, run your forefinger and thumb up them. If something squishes, you have aphids, and you've just taken one useful step in controlling them. Aphids multiply furiously, but they are delicate creatures; in addition to other controls, they are susceptible to plain water or soap spray.

Ants

Ants seldom do any real harm in the greenhouse, but you can try not to bring them in. If you do, you will probably bring in only a few workers. Without a queen, they will wander around aimlessly and die. Strange as it sounds, the old story of ants keeping aphids as "ant cows" is true, but if you control the aphids, the ants will be no problem. If they really bother you, mix equal parts of borax and sugar (a teaspoonful or less) in solution and put the mix in a bottle cap. It may take a while, but usually this works. It may not be strictly organic, but it's unlikely to hurt anything but an insect.

Mites or Spider Mites

Mites are arachnids, like spiders, with the nasty habit of sucking juices out of plants instead of eating flies. They are usually red but may be other colors. Often you will notice their webs before you see the creatures or notice their damage, but don't confuse them with real spider webs. Threads from mites just sort of wander from stem to stem or leaf to leaf without catching anything.

Fig. 32. The tiny spider mite, although a close relative of the beneficial spider, will harm your plants.

Mites can be a stubborn problem. Sometimes a hard stream of water will work. If all else fails, and you don't want to throw out all the plants, you can buy good mites that eat the bad mites.

Whiteflies

Whiteflies, like aphids, are sapsuckers, almost never a problem in the garden but sometimes a real nuisance in the greenhouse. Clouds of tiny white bugs, which upon close inspection resemble little moths, rise from the plant when you disturb it. Use soap solution repeatedly, and be sure to do the undersides of the leaves.

Scale Insects

Scale looks like a disease, but it's an insect that moves so slowly that the motion is indetectable, making it resemble a bump on a stem, with a wax scale covering and protecting it. Control it by wiping stems gently with cotton moistened with rubbing alcohol, using alcohol in a mister, or spraying with a soap solution.

Fig. 33. Scale is a harmful insect that looks like a lump on a leaf or stem.

Mealybugs

The mealybug is a relative of the scale insect, but it moves fast enough that you know it's an insect. It usually looks white and furry. The treatment for scale works equally well on mealybugs on stems or leaves.

Another kind of mealybug attacks roots. Hope you don't get it; if you do, bare-root the plant and use the above treatments, or throw it away. There are also root aphids. Pray you don't get these (I never have), but if you do, follow the same procedure.

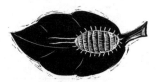

Fig. 34. Mealybugs are ugly in appearance and harmful to your plants.

Thrips

There are pear thrips, citrus thrips, and many other kinds of thrips, but the only ones you are likely to encounter in the greenhouse are onion thrips, which, oddly enough, may also attack carnations or mums. Thrips are something like aphids in appearance and habits, but they are longer, usually darker, and move much faster. You may see the black specks they leave behind before you see them. Soap solution or pepper spray will usually take care of them.

Rootworms

Various kinds of tiny worms attack the roots of cabbages and related plants, like radishes. Carrots aren't related, but they too have a rootworm, or maggot, which is a more appropriate name, since it is the larva of a small fly. The adult female lands near the stem of the plant and lays its eggs on the soil. The larvae hatch quickly and burrow into the soil and then into the root of the plant. It is unlikely that you will encounter these indoors, unless you bring in soil that contains the larvae.

Rootworms are a minor nuisance in radishes and carrots—you can cut them out and eat the rest—but they kill cabbage, broccoli, and similar seedlings by eating too much of the root. If you are the rare greenhouser who grows these plants indoors, and if you are unlucky enough to have these pests, slit a 3-inch square of tar paper or heavy plastic in such a way that you can slip it around the stem of the seedling and have the protective square lie on the soil all around the plant. If that fails, throw out all the infested soil and the plants.

Fungus Gnats

Adult fungus gnats look like fruit flies. I haven't found that they do much harm, but you may have a different experience. The larvae can hurt roots and, in unusual cases, leaves. One authority told me that larvae can be drowned by putting an infested pot in a pail of water for six hours. On the other hand, fungus gnats are a sign of overwatering, so another cure is to dry out the plant as thoroughly as possible, then scrape off the top inch of soil and replace it.

Earwigs and Sow Bugs

Most people have seen these creatures, perhaps without knowing what they were. Earwigs are brown insects with nasty-looking pincers on their rear ends. In spite of their appearance, they are very unlikely to hurt you. Sow bugs, sometimes called wood lice, have many legs, look something like a tiny armadillo, and curl up into a ball when threatened. Neither does much harm; both live in and eat rotten wood, although they may eat a bit of your plants in a pinch. They are night feeders. If they are a problem, leave a piece of board in a greenhouse bed. They will hide under this when the sun comes up, and you can dispose of them.

Snails and Slugs

These gastropods are not common in the greenhouse. The most common control is to put beer in a jar lid and leave it on the soil. They will crawl into it and drown, but they'll die happy. These creatures won't crawl across any gritty or chemical substance. A barrier of wood ashes, lime, or any similar material will keep them away from an area. Salt sprinkled on slugs will destroy them most horribly.

OTHER CREATURES

In my experience, dogs are seldom as much of a nuisance in the garden or the greenhouse as cats. Your pet cat, if you have one, should be barred from the greenhouse. Cats are curious; they will jump up on flats and knock over small pots. Worse, they consider any small expanse of soil to be one more delightful litter box. Cat manure is not generally regarded as desirable anywhere in the garden; the cat usually deposits it where it will do the most harm in the greenhouse. Oh, one more thing: If a greenhouse has plastic glazing, cats love to climb to the top of the structure, then descend by digging their claws into the plastic and sliding down backward.

I have no experience with or information about other mammals in the greenhouse. I presume if mice, or worse, rats get in they can find cozy nesting places and wreak havoc. Old-fashioned traps, baited with old-fashioned cheese, are the best way of getting rid of them.

There are hundreds of other harmful creatures; those above are the ones most commonly found in greenhouses. If you're troubled by something else, and you're reasonably sure it's eating your plants, catch one and take it to your county cooperative extension office or agent. Preserve it whole in rubbing alcohol; agents take a dim view of being asked to diagnose a squashed mess.

DISEASES

There is not a great deal the organic gardener can do about disease in the greenhouse, except to practice hygiene and strive for strong, healthy plants, which are highly resistant to both disease and insects. Diseases are commonly carried by insects; control the insects and you control the disease. Diseases also come into your greenhouse in soil, on plants, and on seeds. Quality seed houses try very hard not to sell you seeds that carry disease, but it happens. The disease is seldom fatal, however.

Damping-Off

Damping-off is the most common greenhouse disease. If a few tiny seedlings out of a large group lie down and refuse to get up, it may be a case of damping-off. In my experience, this just eliminates the weaklings;

the disease never spreads to the rest. If you seem to have epidemics of it, start seeds only in commercial potting soil specifically designed for this purpose. If you still have it, write a nasty letter to the soil producer and don't buy his kind again.

The problem may, however, be in the seed. Buy good seed. If you have a serious problem, follow the procedure for tainted soil. How can you tell which is at fault? If everything damps off, it is the soil. If only one kind of plant does it, it is the seed. You may be a greenhouser for years and never experience any real problem with this condition, which is not one disease, but several similar ones.

A few plants may experience something like damping-off after they are quite well grown. Pansies and petunias are particularly subject to this, but it will only happen if you grow them repeatedly in the same soil, which of course would never happen in your greenhouse.

Mildews

Powdery mildew, downy mildew, and similar problems are diseases associated with too much moisture or humidity. Space plants so that air can circulate. If you can't bottom water, try very hard to water the soil without getting the leaves wet or splashing them.

Many diseases are specific to one plant or a group of plants. For example, tomatoes and some other Solanaceae are subject to a whole host of diseases: verticillium wilt, fusarium wilt, tobacco mosaic virus, and others. The solution to this problem, with tomatoes or other plants, is to choose varieties described as resistant to these problems.

If you practice good greenhouse hygiene, it is unlikely that you will have an epidemic of plant disease. If you do, your only recourse is to throw out all the soil and thoroughly clean and sterilize pots, flats, tools, and everything else. Throw the infected soil in the woods or on a remote part of your property. Don't worry about it; nature will soon take care of it.

If you take the above advice seriously and follow the procedures outlined, the likelihood of your experiencing serious problems with insects or disease is remote. Most of the plants that die in your greenhouse will die at your hand, from overwatering, underwatering, overfertilizing, or because you drop them headfirst on a hard floor. Even then, it's astonishing how many plants will survive these mishaps.

PART II

Starting Plants for Transplanting Outdoors

Types and Sources
of Seeds

Last summer, my six-year-old grandson was helping me plant seeds. I chose radishes as the seeds for him to plant. Though bean seeds are good for kids to work with, especially in school experiments in which they can watch the seed unfold behind glass, outdoors, radish seeds, which are reasonably large, germinate more rapidly than almost anything else, and just about never fail, seem more appropriate.

Chris was mystified by the small spheres. "Is everything in there?" he asked. "The roots, the leaves, what you eat?" I explained as best I could to a first-grader about seed leaves and true leaves, water and nutrients. I couldn't help thinking how blasé we gardeners become about the miracle of life contained in a seed.

It's impossible to describe every kind of seed, but it may be helpful to learn about a few of the common ones. The Bible says that the mustard seed is the smallest seed. I don't wish to get into a religious controversy, but the Bible is, in this small matter, wrong, as most greenhouse gardeners know. Many seeds, poppy, for instance, are smaller. Be careful opening a package of wormwood or chamomile seed. That dust that just blew away was the seed. How large can a seed be? Think peach pit, or even coconut.

VEGETABLES

Some people eat nasturtiums; some won't touch parsnips. Squashes and pumpkins were originally grown, by native South Americans, for their seeds; the rest was thrown away. Squash blossoms are a culinary delight in parts of Europe. Most of us just eat the squash fruit, and some of us won't do that. All categorization is arbitrary. What we call vegetables are a small number of plants that most people eat. The most common ones are listed here.

All varieties recommended in this chapter are for starting indoors and transplanting into the garden; varieties recommended for growing to maturity indoors are listed in the appropriate chapters. Selecting the correct variety can be very important in growing greenhouse vegetables; with garden vegetables, it is more a matter of taste. Soil, rainfall, and sunlight are more important in the garden than variety.

Brassica Varieties

Mustard is in the *Brassica* genus, which includes cabbage, broccoli, and cauliflower, as well as turnips and radishes. Brassica seeds are typically perfect spheres, although they vary in size. This makes it easy to roll them from a creased sheet of paper but harder to get only one to roll out at a time.

When you grow your own broccoli for the first time, you receive a pleasant surprise. After you cut the main head, the plant keeps producing, and producing, side sprouts. They aren't as big as the first head, but a half dozen or so will give you a pint of frozen broccoli. There is a kind of broccoli called Italian sprouting, which is supposed to produce more side sprouts, but I find it no better in this regard than Comet or Emperor, and its main head is never as large or firm.

Cabbages have been bred to the point that some mature in less than two months, while others take about four. This means that you can start all your cabbage seeds at the same time and have cabbage all summer.

In fact, I haven't found much advantage in starting any of the Brassica seeds at intervals. Broccoli pretty much lasts forever after it matures, and Brussels sprouts can be started as early as the rest. Cabbages that take longer store better. Beware: Unless you really love cabbage or make kraut, a few cabbages go a long, long way. Primo is a good early cabbage; any of the Danish ballheads are good long-season ones. Jade Cross Brussels sprouts do well for us.

Cucurbit Varieties

Almost everyone knows what a squash or pumpkin seed looks like. These are *Cucurbita,* or cucurbits (pronounced "kyew-CUR-bits"), a group that also includes melons, cucumbers, and gourds. Although the seeds vary in size, all are much larger than mustard, and most have one rounded and one pointed end.

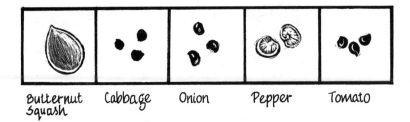

Butternut Squash • Cabbage • Onion • Pepper • Tomato

Fig. 35. An assortment of vegetable seeds.

We like yellow crookneck summer squash and Milano zucchini, and prefer Waltham butternut winter squash to any acorn squash. Delicata is a small, tasty winter squash, but it tastes no better than butternut and won't keep as long. Most cucumbers are fine; you may want to grow a regular variety, like Longfellow or Straight Eight, and a pickling variety, like Boston Pickling. Blonde and lemon cukes are for people who rank novelty above other qualities.

Solanaceae

Tomatoes, peppers, and eggplant are members of the family Solanaceae. So are potatoes, tobacco, and deadly nightshade, but you probably won't be starting those in your greenhouse. It's worth noting, however, that their relationship to poisonous plants means that some parts of these vegetable plants not normally eaten, such as the foliage, can make you quite ill. These seeds are coin-shaped—that is, round and flat—and often have a little pointy bump on them. They are easy to handle with fingers or a tiny pair of tweezers.

Tomato Varieties. Many people who don't grow anything else grow tomatoes, which is why seed companies offer, at best, one or two kinds of turnip or parsnip seeds and hundreds of different tomato seeds. A company called Totally Tomatoes publishes a catalog containing nothing but tomatoes, peppers, and related plants like tomatillos. It lists over three hundred items, of which more than two hundred are tomatoes.

In addition to red, you can grow pink, purple, "blue," yellow, or orange tomatoes, if you choose to, or tomatoes ranging in size from $3/4$ inch in diameter to a variety that grew a world-record tomato weighing over 7 pounds. (The catalog doesn't say how it tasted.) Among regular tomatoes we like are Burpee's Supersteak, Better Boy, and an old French variety, new to this country, called St. Pierre. For information on special kinds of tomatoes for greenhouse growing, see chapter 15.

Sweet Pepper Varieties. Bell Boy and California Wonder are well-known sweet green peppers. Both have produced satisfactorily for me. The latter grows a few inches taller (both produce plants about 2 feet tall) and requires about five fewer days to mature, on average. Red Beauty is a new pepper that is said to turn red sooner than the above two; I couldn't see much difference when I tried it. Corno di Toro (Horn of the Bull) is a sweet Italian pepper, good for frying, shaped vaguely as the name indicates.

Hot Pepper Varieties. There are far more varieties of hot peppers than of sweet ones. I have grown all of the following, listed in order from hottest to mildest.

Cayennes are among the hottest peppers available. The bush usually grows 12 to 18 inches high and is very decorative, with long, slim, curved fruit that turns red very early. A small amount of dried cayenne will add a lot of bite to any dish.

Jalapeños come in a variety of "heats," but most will burn an Anglo's mouth. They are easy to grow, shaped somewhat like a small sausage, and always stay green in my experience. Ancho is a Mexican poblano-type pepper, shaped like a bell but pointier. It is considered fairly mild by pepper

Fig. 36. A Corno di Toro pepper plant.

lovers. I find it hot enough. If you grow both Ancho and Corno di Toro, label carefully, or you may forget which is which.

Hungarian Hot Wax is a pretty pepper that turns yellow quite early in its growth cycle. Even I find these reasonably mild, usable in salads. An elderly Hungarian lady of my acquaintance stuffs these with sauerkraut and pickles them. I have pickled them without the kraut.

Caution: If you are growing hot peppers for the first time, beware. They can be far more powerful than the novice would believe. If you handle cayennes or jalapeños with your unprotected fingers and then rub eyes, nose, or lips, it will make you cry. In an extreme case, you may have to visit the emergency room.

The pungency of a given type may vary greatly from specimen to specimen, depending on soil, climate, and other factors. It may even vary from one end of the pepper to the other. Seeds are usually the hottest parts.

Umbelliferae and Compositae

Parsley, celery, and fennel, which you may start in the greenhouse, and carrots and parsnips, which you won't, are members, along with Queen Anne's lace, of the family Umbelliferae. Seeds are fairly small (except for fennel), pointed on one end, and sometimes slightly curved into a comma shape. Most lettuces, romaine, endive, and so forth are in the family Compositae, along with daisies, chrysanthemums, and many other flowers. The seeds are like those of parsley but smaller, straighter, and more delicate and light. They may be black or whitish. Umbellifer seeds are hard to separate in order to plant just one in each cell; composite seeds are impossible.

Lettuce Varieties. Red Sails is a great red lettuce. A slightly improved form of Black-Seeded Simpson, which is over one hundred years old, is Elite. Stick to these over Johnny-come-lately's. Tom Thumb is a good butterhead that takes no more time than looseleaf. Parris Island Cos is romaine, which will usually stand more heat without bolting. I've had fair luck with Ithaca head lettuce. Summertime is a cross between Ithaca and Salinas, said to be superior to its parents. I haven't found it better than Ithaca.

Parsley and Celery Varieties. To most people, parsley is just parsley, but an Italian (flat-leaved) variety called Prezzemolo Gigante is much tastier and grows much larger than other parsleys we have tried. Celery comes in self-blanching and not. I grow "not" and don't bother to try to blanch it; it is chewy but tasty that way. Self-blanching produces smaller, less healthy, and less tasty celery, but it is white.

Beets and Relatives

Beets have the botanical name *Beta* because some botanists thought the seed looked like the Greek letter *B*. Swiss chard is also a *Beta;* spinach is *Spinacia* but is a close relative of beets and chard. It can be said with almost total certainty that you won't start carrots indoors, but you may be surprised to find that commercial growers and gardeners who sell at farmers' markets often start beets and Swiss chard in a greenhouse to get an early jump on the season. You may want to also.

Beet "seeds" are large and spherical but nubbly, not smooth like cabbage seeds. This makes them very easy to handle. That's the good news.

The bad news is that what we call a beet seed is, in fact, a beet fruit, containing several seeds. That means that several beet seedlings will come up close together, and all but the strongest will have to be removed. Seedsmen have succeeded in producing seeds from which only one beet will grow. Monogram and Monopoly are two such kinds. Whether or not it is worthwhile to use such seed in the garden, it is probably a good idea in the greenhouse. Other than that, we find no great difference among ordinary beet varieties, although you may want to grow a long narrow, yellow, or red-and-yellow striped kind.

Alliums

Onions are alliums, which means that they are a variety of lily. The group also includes asparagus, garlic, and shallots. The last two are usually started from bulbs or sets; asparagus is started from roots or rhizomes. Onions can be started from sets, but they, along with leeks, chives, and garlic chives, can be grown from seed started indoors early. Onions grown from seed have several advantages over those grown from sets, one of the most obvious being cost. Seeds of these plants are a bit bigger than mustard, quite black, and irregularly shaped.

It is moderately difficult to plant one such seed in a cell; most gardeners don't try, but just scatter them in something like a rectangular plastic container 3 by 4 by 6 inches. Since onions are bulbs, you can't hurt them later when separating them to plant out, as long as you make sure they are thoroughly wet. And since they are monocots, you can't hurt them by cutting off the tops. In fact, some gardeners prune the roots and tops of leeks before setting them out, although I've never seen much advantage to this practice.

We like yellow Spanish onions; you may want a long-storage white variety. Large American Flag is a good variety of leek.

HERBS

Many herbs, such as basil and lemon balm, are in the mint family; a tip-off is their square stems. Mint itself is seldom grown from seed; you acquire a plant divided from a friend's stock and have mint forever after. Other members of the mint family, however, are easily grown from seeds, which are round, black, and usually small but not tiny. Dill, parsley and many other herbs are in the family Umbelliferae, described above. Chives, garlic chives, and garlic are alliums. Many specific herbs are described in detail in chapter 16.

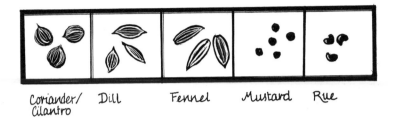

Coriander/   Dill   Fennel   Mustard   Rue
Cilantro

Fig. 37. An assortment of herb seeds.

FLOWERS

It would be impossible to list here all the kinds of seeds that are planted to produce flowers. One book on flower gardening lists about 150 names, from ageratum to zinnia, and many varieties under each name. And those are just annuals.

Chapters 12 and 17 discuss some of the best varieties for growing to maturity indoors. Most of these are also the varieties I like best for starting inside and transplanting to the garden.

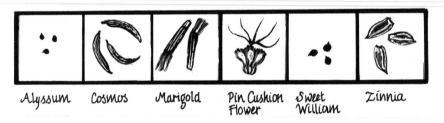

Alyssum   Cosmos   Marigold   Pin Cushion Sweet   Zinnia
                                Flower   William

Fig. 38. An assortment of flower seeds.

SEED COMPANIES

The Shakers were a religious group of the eighteenth and nineteenth centuries. Not many are left, because among the many practices forbidden to them was sex, although they did adopt children. They left us beautiful furniture and music and modern seed marketing. The Shakers were the first to put up the seed they had for sale in packets.

There are hundreds, if not thousands, of seed companies in the United States. A few of them are listed in the Appendix. Many sell primarily to farmers or commercial growers. Some sell nothing but beans, or corn, or flowers, or vegetables. Most cater to home gardeners like you. All of them will cheerfully send you catalogs forever if they have your name and address. With a minimum of trouble, you can receive two or three dozen catalogs filled with glowing descriptions of flowers, fruits, vegetables, and herbs, which will arrive at the right time to brighten the dead of winter.

All seedsmen are by no means equally reliable or useful for your purpose. If you have any kind of problem with seed, such as damping-off or very poor germination, or total lack thereof, write to the company. Most will be glad to hear from you and will replace the seed (which probably won't do you any good until next season). Be morally certain that the fault wasn't yours—that the starting medium was good and the seeds got enough but not too much moisture and warmth. If you are sure, and you are not satisfied with the response you get, never buy seed from them again.

Strange as it may seem, if you don't buy seeds by mail, you might do better to buy them at a small local hardware store or garden supply store than at a giant discount department store. The price may be lower at the giant, but there is a greater chance that the seed was not grown in this country. Some of the seed at the hardware store may

Fig. 39. These modern seed packets are a far cry from the ones the Shakers sold.

also have been grown abroad, but it is somewhat more likely to have been grown in the United States and less likely to have been grown in the Southern Hemisphere. Seed grown in South America, where the seasons are reversed, may be six months older than seed grown in Europe or the United States.

The vast majority of American seed suppliers do not raise seed themselves but buy it wholesale, make it up into retail packages, and sell it to you. This means that the Burpee Supersteak tomato seed you buy from Company X is probably exactly the same as that from Company Y. (If they call it Burpee, that probably means that Burpee still owns the patent.)

There can be a tremendous disparity in price for the same seed from two different companies. Compare catalog listings carefully, particularly with regard to amount; other things being equal, buy from the company with the lowest prices. You may notice a relationship between the splendor and glossiness of the catalog and the price of the seed.

Some seed catalogs provide a great deal of very useful information and advice on growing the plants listed; others don't. You'll have to decide how much such information is worth to you. It is probably unethical to use the information in one grower's catalog and buy your seed from another, but it is also probably a common practice.

SEED QUALITY

By law, all seed sold in the United States must have certain information on the packet, including variety, an identifying number, and the words "Packed for 1998" or some other year. "Packed for 1998" doesn't always mean "grown in 1997," although that would usually be the case. State and federal authorities check from time to time; if seed "packed for 1998," when tested, doesn't have an appropriate germination rate, the company is punished. Some states, notably Pennsylvania and Maine, have stricter laws in this regard than the federal government, so it's probably slightly better to buy seed from companies that do business in these states. In the last analysis, the reputation of the seed company is your best guide.

Note: Seed houses are accustomed to dealing with home gardeners who plant seeds outdoors. Be sure that when sending in an order, you make it crystal clear several times that you want these seeds not later than a certain date, for greenhouse planting. They won't have too much trouble getting tomato and pepper seeds to you in January or February, but if you want to start seeds after July and before January, you will find it much safer to order them the preceding spring. You may, on the other hand, want to take advantage of sales at the local hardware or garden supply store; they often unload this year's seeds in August at bargain-basement prices. The catalog house would probably send you seeds the same age in October or November.

QUANTITY

Sometimes it is difficult to determine from the catalog how much seed is in a packet. Most greenhousers don't need very much seed; be sure you aren't paying for a lot more seed than you can use. Though some seed will keep for a few years if handled right, the ideal arrangement is to buy and pay for just the amount you need each year. At first, the thirty hybrid tomato seeds in a packet may not look like many, but even if you give some away, do you really want to start more than twenty Viva tomato plants?

TREATED AND PELLETIZED SEED

Many companies sell treated seed, which has been dipped in a chemical to repel diseases, insects, and sometimes pests like crows or mice. It is often recommended that such seed be used in cold soil in spring, when disease can be a real problem. Be sure that you are getting what you want. Organic purists don't use treated seed, and there is little need for it indoors, where the soil should always be nice and warm.

Commercial growers also use pelletized seed. Seed companies have developed a way to enclose seeds in pellets, which may incorporate enzymes, tiny amounts of fertilizer, or similar growth-stimulating material, but the main reason to buy pelletized seed is that it can be used in a mechanical planter. You might find pelletization handy with seeds like carrot, which are hard to handle (and aren't started in the greenhouse anyway), but you would be paying a great deal for the convenience.

FADS

Seed companies, or more often the seed growers they buy from, are always experimenting and hybridizing. Over the years, this has resulted in the production of better plants that are easier to grow, with bigger blooms or fruit, greater resistance to disease, and other good qualities. It has also had some negative side effects. Many companies, whether they sell seeds or soap, try to get you to buy their product each year by coming up with something "bigger and better." New isn't always better, nor is hybrid. If you plant hybrids (and I do, in some cases), one thing it means is that you won't be able to harvest your own seed; you'll have to buy it from the company again next year. To be fair, it also means, often, that your plant won't die of disease.

Black-Seeded Simpson lettuce is still one of the best. Sweet 100 cherry tomatoes have been around about twenty years, but now the seed growers tell us that Sweet Million are even better. I still prefer Sweet 100s, but some companies don't even stock the seed anymore. Here's a rule of thumb you can try: Don't buy the splendid new varieties featured in the front of the catalog, with glossy color pictures. Wait a couple of years, until they are in their proper place, in the alphabetical listing.

HARVESTING SEED

Many gardeners, especially those interested in the preservation and use of heirloom flowers and vegetables, save their own seed. You can use seed you have harvested the previous fall, but you must take certain precautions. You have to know, beyond doubt, that none of the plants from which you take seeds are hybrids, which will usually not breed true. This is one of the many reasons that everything grown in the greenhouse or the garden must be accurately, thoroughly, and indelibly labeled.

Flowers from which I have successfully collected seeds include petunias, poppies, marigolds, cosmos, sweet William, nasturtiums, zinnias, and many, many others. Vegetable seeds that may be harvested include peas, beans, corn, tomatoes, peppers (but most corn plants nowadays, and many tomatoes and peppers, are hybrids), and, of all things, radishes. Most of us forget to pull up the odd radish; a couple months later it will have sent up a stalk 2 feet or more high and developed small seedpods, which contain perfectly usable seed. I'm not proud of it, but I've even gathered seed from lettuce that I neglected too long.

Some plants, such as tomatoes and peas, are self-pollinating in the sense that they are not pollinated by insects. Others, such as squash, are pollinated by bees or other insects. Seeds from the latter are seldom gathered for future use. If you grew only one kind of squash, it wasn't a hybrid, you had no other gardens near yours, and there weren't any wild cucumbers nearby, it might possibly be worth saving squash seeds, but those are a lot of ifs.

Gardeners argue a great deal about the way in which cucurbits may be cross-fertilized. If you plant, for example, pumpkins anywhere near zucchini, bees will travel between the plants. According to botanists, the fruit this year will be fine, but seeds from this fruit will next year produce a "zumpkin" or "pucchini," usually monstrous. Worse, there is a wild cucurbit that often springs up near gardens and may cross with squash or cucumbers. The fruit of such a cross could even be poisonous. For this reason it is usually unwise to save seed from cucurbits.

Although scientists say it can't happen, many gardeners swear that they have had cucurbits that hybridized in the first year. That is, they planted fresh, new, store-bought cucumber seed and harvested monsters.

These gardeners separate cucurbits as widely as possible in the garden. Some gardeners are convinced, in spite of botanists, that hot and sweet peppers planted near each other will all produce mildly hot fruit. I planted golden acorn squash and got monsters; instead of attributing it to cross-fertilization, I believed the scientists and wrote a nasty letter to the seed company.

The reason that gardeners harvest seed from many more flowers than vegetables is simple: We grow most vegetables for their leaves, roots, or stems; we do everything we can to prevent their going to seed. Vegetables grown for fruits, such as tomatoes, or seeds, such as beans, are the exception. Since many herbs are grown for their seeds, and most aren't hybrids, their seeds can be harvested and reused. I use my own harvested dill, caraway, coriander, mustard, and several other herb seeds, unless I want to try a new variety.

The technique for seed harvesting is not difficult. You already know where the seed is on beans, peas, or dill. Mustard and radishes, along with many other plants, like the little-known herb fenugreek, produce long, thin, tapered pods that contain a surprising number of small, round seeds. Harvest these when they begin to become dry; if necessary, finish drying them in the greenhouse (see chapter 16).

You will soon learn the seed-producing cycle of various flowers. Obviously, you can't deadhead (remove dead and dying blooms from) flowers from which you wish to save seed. Instead, when the bloom is thoroughly dead and dry, remove it, take off the petals, and save the seedpod, in whatever form it occurs. If you wait too long, the flower will achieve its goal of strewing its seeds around the garden. This is one area in which a little experience will teach you more than ten thousand words.

The tomato may present some difficulty in the saving of its seed. The usual recommendation is this: Allow a few tomatoes to become overripe on the vine. (Seeds from normally ripe or underripe tomatoes, or tomatoes that have become overripe on the kitchen counter, will not usually germinate.) Squeeze seeds from such a tomato into some kind of container; they will of necessity be accompanied by a certain amount of pulp and juice. Let the mess stand on a windowsill until it begins to ferment (you'll know). Discard the fluid and the seeds that float. Take the seeds that have sunk to the bottom, and spread them out on blotting paper to dry in the sun.

The above procedure is supposed to kill disease that is present on the seeds. One expert gardener just squeezes the seeds out of the tomato onto a thick layer of newspaper and dries them in a sunny window, and has had no problem with this method. If you've had experience with "volunteer" tomato plants springing up in bean rows or among the petunias in your garden, you know most tomato seed will be perfectly healthy without any complicated treatment. In fairness to the reader, I will state that I buy new tomato seed each year, although I grow cayenne peppers each year from seed harvested from my peppers the preceding fall.

SEED STORAGE

Whether you have leftover seed from a commercial supplier or seed you have harvested, it should be stored in the same way, in a cool, dry, dark place. Some books recommend sealing each type of seed in a plastic bag and storing them all in the freezer. If you are a typical gardener, such a procedure would take up far too much space in the freezer.

The important practices are to make sure seed is bone dry, seal it in a jar or bag, and keep it out of the light and in the coolest place possible. For many of us, this is the basement; an attic or an unused spare room is also possible. Many of us don't get around to removing seed from the greenhouse as soon as we're through with it for that year. Let's face it—you're not going to start any more peppers or tomatoes after May 1. Get that seed into a sealed jar or bag and into a cool, dry, dark place as soon as you're through using it. If you don't, not only will you waste money, but far worse, you'll run the risk of planting two dozen seeds and not having a single one germinate.

Many nongarden products that are shipped from catalog houses include in the package a very small container, boldly labeled something like this: "Warning! Desiccant. Do not eat. Unfit for human consumption." A desiccant is a drying agent. Save all of these and put them in with your seeds that are stored in tightly sealed containers; they will help keep them dry. Some gardeners say that powdered milk will function as a desiccant.

SEED LIFE EXPECTANCIES

Sometimes it seems as though gardening experts can't agree on anything, except that gardening is a splendid activity. One book I have says beet seed will keep a year; another says five. Perhaps the first author didn't store the seed very well. Based on experience, the best advice I can give is this: Parsnip seed, which you'll never plant in the greenhouse anyway, is only good brand new (and even then, it's balky). Parsley and various onion-type seeds will last two or three years. Most other kinds of seeds will keep about five years, *if* they are properly stored. Unless you bought way too much of some kind of seed and can't bear to throw it away, it's better in most cases to buy fresh seed every year. For one thing, even though stale seed germinates, it may produce far less vigorous plants than fresh seed would have.

Starting Seeds

Few thrills in life, except perhaps watching the birth of one's child, compare with putting seeds in soil and seeing, a week or more later, the tiny seedlings heaving their heads above the soil. Fortunately for gardeners, this process is a lot cheaper, less time-consuming, and certainly less painful than giving birth.

REASONS *NOT* TO START PLANTS

There are dozens of reasons why you should start your own tomato and petunia plants rather than buying them, but first let's look at a few reasons not to. You shouldn't start seeds inside if you don't like to get your hands wet and muddy or get dirt under your fingernails, or if you don't want your greenhouse to become fairly messy and dirty. If you're that neat, you're probably not a gardener anyway.

A much more important consideration is this: If you start seeds inside, you won't be able to leave home from approximately February to April for more than forty-eight hours at a time. If you can find an extremely knowledgeable and reliable plant-sitter, fine; otherwise you may come back to find hundreds of tiny plants dead and all your hard work wasted. A plant-sitter should be at least as capable and responsible as a baby-sitter. Remember, babies can cry if they are thirsty or too hot; your plants cannot.

REASONS TO START PLANTS

Reasons *to* start your own seeds are legion. It is vastly cheaper than buying plants at the garden supply store or supermarket, and the plants you raise will be, at least in some ways, much better. They will not be as crowded or as leggy—tall, spindly, and scrawny—because you will have transplanted them at least once before setting them out. They may be healthier in other ways as well, because they have received proper sunlight and watering and the minimal necessary amount of natural, organic fertilizer. They won't have been artificially forced in order to look good for the first couple of weeks—but possibly not very good thereafter.

You will have a much wider selection of varieties; commercial growers start what is convenient to them and familiar to the vast majority of customers, not what you want. You can start heirloom tomatoes or white eggplant, if you wish. You probably won't find cayenne pepper or chamomile plants at the store, but you can surely find those seeds in the catalogs.

Furthermore, you can raise plants free of chemical pesticides or fertilizers. Many greenhouses are conscientious and careful about the use of chemicals; many, unfortunately, are not. Plants you buy, especially at a supermarket or discount store, may have been imported from out of state, or even out of the country, and may have been dosed with substances or amounts that would be illegal for a local grower. If you grow them yourself, you will know what was used on them.

The best reason of all, though, is to see tiny seedlings appear and, under your care, turn into huge plants by the end of the summer. Of course, it's fun to see beans you planted in the garden pop up all together one day, but to find a tiny, tiny petunia one morning, transplant it three weeks later, when it is still minuscule, and get beautiful blooms all summer is even better.

WHICH PLANTS TO START
What you will grow in your greenhouse depends partly on you and partly on nature. Most gardeners don't think it's worth their time to start plants indoors that grow very large or are grown in very large quantities, such as beans, corn, and potatoes, but there is no reason you can't start such plants or grow them to maturity there, if that is your wish, although you'd better have a big greenhouse for corn.

If, like the vast majority of us, you start things in the greenhouse for later transplanting, there are some plants that you probably shouldn't tackle. As a beginning gardener, I was taught that certain plants can't be transplanted. It would probably be more accurate to say that some plants are very easy to transplant, some moderately difficult, and some nearly impossible.

Some plants, notably the brassicas, actually seem to grow better if they are moved once or twice rather than left to grow to maturity where the seed was planted. Some, like parsley, are moderately difficult to transplant successfully, usually because they have long taproots and die if much of the root is broken off. Most cucurbits are considered difficult to transplant, because, although they don't have long taproots, they can't survive the loss of many rootlets. If you follow the directions in chapter 9, however, you will have no difficulty with any of these plants.

Some common plants have roots like parsley, only more so, and are not worth trying to transplant. These include carrots, dill, coriander, and savory. You will discover others for yourself, but it is worth noting that many of these plants are in the family Umbelliferae.

Some perennials are seldom grown from seed. Roses are in this category. On the other hand, although it is often recommended that perennial herbs like rosemary be grown from cuttings, I have had success growing them from seed. A commonsense rule of thumb is this: If the seed is purchasable, presumably you can grow a plant from it, although everything isn't as easy as radishes.

TIMING

Beginners often start plants too early. Directions on the seed package say something like, "Start indoors eight weeks before the average date of the last frost in your area." Unfortunately, the last frost sometimes decides to come before or after the average date.

You'll learn by trial and error, but here are a few tips: Tomatoes are almost always too big before you're ready to stick them in the ground. Peppers and eggplant grow more slowly. The ground should be good and warm, and nights should not go much below 50 degrees, before you put in any Solanaceae. They won't freeze if it's colder, but they'll just sit there, refuse to grow, and look at you accusingly. In my experience, of these three, tomatoes will stand the most cold, eggplant the least.

Brassicas shoot up like weeds in the greenhouse. The good news is that you can and should rush the season in setting them out, since they prefer cool growing conditions.

Two general rules will stand you in good stead. First, the smaller the seed, the earlier you should plant it. You won't go far wrong if you start the tiniest seeds first and the biggest last. Petunias, Canterbury bells,

lavender, oregano, and many others, especially parsley and rosemary, will seem as
though they are never coming up and will
grow very slowly at first.

Second, plants that will stand a little
frost in the fall can be set out earlier (and
therefore started earlier) than items like
basil, which swoons and turns black at the
first cool breeze of September. Whether they
are biennials, perennials, or hardier annuals,
such plants often have tiny seeds that germinate poorly. You should start them quite
early. Unless you live south of New York
City, however, you probably shouldn't start
anything before February 1, and April 1 is
early enough to start tomatoes, zinnias,
marigolds, and similar large-seeded, quick-

Fig. 40. Canterbury bells.

growing plants. This rule, of course, doesn't apply to plants that are going
to be grown entirely in the greenhouse, not set into the garden.

For the home gardener, unlike the commercial grower, starting plants
too early or too late is not a disaster. If they're too late, just set them out
later; they'll probably catch up. If they're too early, keep repotting them in
bigger pots; you'll wind up putting monsters into the ground and being
the first on your block to have zinnias in bloom or tomatoes to eat. Note,
however, that fruiting plants that have buds on them before they are set
out never do as well in the long run as those that do not. Many gardeners
look for tomato plants at the commercial greenhouse or supermarket that
have already blossomed or even have set tiny fruit, but these are actually
the worst ones to buy.

There are a few tricks for slowing down growth, once the seeds have
germinated. Keep the plants as dry and cold as you dare, and delay repotting them. But give them plenty of light; too little light will make them
leggy, not stunt their growth.

OVERPRODUCTION

Next to starting too early or too late, the most common problem is over-
production. You will undoubtedly find yourself with more cosmos or sage

on your hands than you can possibly use. People whose eyes are bigger than their gardens always plant too many seeds. If you *do* wind up with too much of something, give it to a friend, trade with someone else who starts seeds, or *throw it in the compost!* If you can't be ruthless in thinning and culling, you'll never make a good gardener, but having a few excess plants will make you very popular with fellow gardeners.

SALES

If you plan to make your greenhouse pay for itself by selling your surplus production, think long and hard. In many states, laws rigorously control such sale. Often the laws would make you do just what you don't want to do, such as use chemical pesticides. Selling plants at a roadside stand or farmers' market is like everything else anybody does for money: very hard and frustrating work. Sometimes a good compromise solution is to sell plants for the benefit of a church or other charity; the customers are usually less picky and the state will probably stay off your back. But of course you won't make any money.

SELECTING CONTAINERS

Some containers, beds or large pots, are more or less permanent homes for plants. Should you decide to grow very-hard-to-transplant items, such as carrots, indoors, start them in their permanent homes.

Most seedlings, however, will be started in small cells, or pockets, in a multiple-cell pack and transplanted at least once, perhaps twice. The most popular containers for this are plastic six-packs. Every gardener has seen them; commercially grown plants are almost always sold in them. Usually green, sometimes black, they are 5 by 5 inches and have six cells.

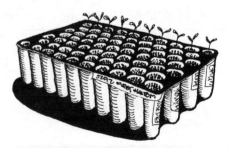

Large flats with many tiny cells are better by far than six-packs for all but the largest seedlings. Some of these have 512 cells in a 16-by-32 pattern; others have slightly larger pockets, 12 across and 22 down. It

Fig. 41. This sixty-seven-cell flat could be used for large seedlings like tomatoes.

may sound quite fussy to work with such small cells, but believe me, it is well worth it in ease of handling and space saved. Both the 512s and the 264s measure about 21 by 10 inches and are designed to fit into the tops of slightly larger plastic flats that will hold water. They come with clear plastic covers that are also designed to fit. You can get all these items from supply houses or beg a couple from a friendly commercial grower.

LABELING

After deciding which size containers to use, lay them out, along with the packets of seed you want to plant. Label the containers with all pertinent information, including the date. Use masking tape and a truly waterproof marker. Do it *before* you get the container wet or fill it with a growing medium. Labeling those tiny rows is a very fussy job. Here are a few helpful tips: You probably don't need to use all the rows; skip one or two every so often. You only need to put the date on once, not on every row. Be inventive about abbreviating, or label the rows A, B, C, and so forth, and write what each code letter stands for in your greenhouse log.

You will soon learn what newborn tomato, petunia, and cabbage plants look like, and even to tell the difference between tomatoes and peppers. The labeling will let you know which tomatoes are Better Boys and which are Vivas. If you are going to use them all in your own garden, it's possible that you don't care, but most gardeners want to be able to tell later which varieties did best for them. It is also essential to know on what date seeds were started. After they are transplanted, the new container label should give the date of transplanting as well as the date of seed starting.

RECORD KEEPING

You will want to keep a greenhouse log, or journal, in which you faithfully record data like the above. You can go into more detail in the journal. Most serious and experienced gardeners keep extensive records. If you don't, you will keep on making the same mistakes every year, starting the tomatoes too early and the eggplant too late, or using a variety of marigold that didn't do well for you or that you didn't like the color of.

If you have a home computer, you can keep a journal on it listing all of the above information. A good trick is to note at the end of the growing season all the things you would like to do differently next year, then transcribe this information in advance into your journal entry for January of that year. You might look back to last year's entries when you are ordering seed and getting ready to start items in the greenhouse; then again, you might not. A journal kept on your home computer might be quite formal, or it might look something like this:

"Friday, February 7th—Some sun yesterday and today, but cold last night and probably tonight. What the weather guy calls seasonable temps. Finally planted a few seeds. Four kinds of peppers and three of tomatoes, essentially four seeds of each. Hope to raise them to fruition inside the greenhouse, keeping them warm with sunny days, furnace heat at night, and electric tape in between, although their average temp will be more like 70 than 85.

"Also, in a big white Styrofoam box, one row spinach, two of radishes, and about five of various lettuces. Most of these to grow to maturity indoors. Tried to plant thinly. Average temp for these is more like 60, cooler at night. Suspect that in the past they have gotten too hot; will try to keep them cool as they mature. Deep box.

"All above new Pinetree seeds; surprisingly few seeds in packet. I see now that hybrid tomatoes claim only fifteen or more per packet, peppers twenty, others more.

"Thursday, 13th—Sun all day. Planted exactly twelve pansy seeds, six in dark, six in light, none covered with dirt. Watered all previous seed plantings with quite warm water. About four tomatoes are up, mostly Sungold. Managing to keep them between 65 and 85 degrees. Lettuce may get too warm, but next few days will be cloudy, or so they say.

"Friday, Valentine's Day—Snow overnight, cold indoors.

"Monday, 17th—Beautiful day weatherwise, about $2^{1}/2$ inches light fluffy snow overnight, but sun just about all day. Most tomatoes now up, no sign of peppers. Can keep flat around 75 to 80 at night and use grow light at same time. 85 on bright sunlit days. *Note:* It is very important *not* to plant peppers and tomatoes in same flat. Peppers should be separate from everything (except possibly eggplant) because they require more intense heat. At this point I would like to keep the little toms cooler and the pepps hotter, but that is impossible. Lettuce, spinach (very small amount), and radishes all up nicely. No sign of pansies. Planted eight boxes leeks and yellow Spanish onions on the 15th, about twenty-five per box, maybe a hundred onions and fifty leeks.

"Saturday, 22nd—Very strange weather, 50s outside yesterday and this morning, clouds & a little sun, showers, quite like April or May.

Everything a mess with mud, etc. Supposed to drop abruptly midafternoon, be 20 tomorrow morning, but probably sunnier next few days.

"Interesting phenomenon: Pansies kept in dark have sprouted; nothing from other kind of pansies, in spite of instructions on label. Will probably have very few. Leeks and onions stubbornly refuse to germinate; there are a few shoots that may be onions or grass. Should look up appropriate temp and lighting. Planted a total of twenty-eight-plus peppers and tomatoes on the 10th or 11th; twenty-one have now sprouted. Looking quite good. Kept heating coil on under them the whole time, practically, with add'l heat from sun at times. Used artificial light some. Read meter today; not a lot of excess electrical use for that.

"Tuesday, Feb. 25th—Bottom watered all seedlings today, transplanted twelve tomatoes, all there were. Leeks showing fairly well, one or two onions. They are slow, perhaps seeds planted too deep. There will be only a very few pansies. Lettuce and radishes may show signs of being too warm, especially the radishes.

"Friday, 28—Last day of Feb, and we are glad to see spring coming, however slowly and muddily. Rain most of yesterday, foggy, above freezing, obviously. Sun came through very slowly this morning. Leeks up well, and more onions. Transplanted all tomatoes to 4-inch pots; peppers are all alone now. Some peppers and tomatoes didn't come up at all, some peppers came up late and died, but I have enough of both. Most everything in greenhouse looks good."

MOISTENING THE SOIL MEDIUM

When you decide the time is right to plant some seeds, select a flat and a water container to go under it. Fill the underlying container with *tepid* water to within about $1/2$ inch of the top. Fill the flat lightly with the right kind of potting soil (see chapter 3). Put it in the water and leave it there until every pocket looks dark and wet. The edge and corner pockets will get wet last; if they stay dry, lift the pack out, add more water, and reinsert it. When all pockets are damp, lift the pack out and let it drain. Good potting soil resists getting wet, but once it is wet, it holds water a long time. Soil tends to pack down; you may have to fill the pockets to the brim after the first watering and repeat the procedure.

Fill all the cells, including the ones you are going to use at a later date or not at all. This helps greatly to keep the cells with seeds in them from drying out.

PLANTING THE SEEDS

Now comes the hard part—and you thought the above parts were hard enough! When each cell is brim-full of wet soil, place exactly one seed on top of the soil in each pocket. Try hard not to put more than one in a cell; it is better to leave a cell empty than to have two or more seeds in it. This is easy with big seeds, like peppers; it is difficult but possible with tiny seeds like petunias. If you are planting anything like wormwood, the seeds of which are simply fine dust, do the best you can.

Fig. 42. With practice, you can learn to tap seeds off a creased piece of paper one at a time.

The more trouble you take with this now, the happier you'll be later, especially at transplanting time. You can use tweezers or toothpicks, but with a little time and practice, you'll develop amazing dexterity at getting just one seed in each pocket.

Tip: Fold and crease a sheet of clean white paper of good quality, then open it. Put the seeds on this. Hold it with one hand and tap it with the other. With practice, you will get very good at having exactly one seed at a time drop from the end of the crease. This works particularly well with seeds like sage or broccoli, which are not tiny, but annoyingly rolly.

Fig. 43. Fine soil to cover seeds is obtained using a simple kitchen strainer.

When all seeds are in place, wet them lightly with a mister or sprayer, then, through a kitchen strainer, dust on potting soil to cover. Press it down with your thumb. For certain seeds, the pressing-down part of the process is very important, so don't ignore it. Follow directions on the seed packet, but in general, cover big seeds, like tomatoes, with $^1/_8$ inch of firmed soil and tiny ones, like petunias, with $^1/_{16}$ inch or less. Commercial growers leave all seeds uncovered except those that will germinate only in the dark, but commercial growers can control the moisture in the soil better than you can. Uncovered seeds can dry out with amazing speed. Some books suggest that it is possible to get seeds too wet, but I have never found that to be so, provided that they are kept sufficiently warm for the first day or so.

Directions on packets can vary a lot. Some seeds, like lettuce, are said to need light to germinate; a rare few like to sprout in the dark. I haven't found that seeds are too fussy about light, if the tiny ones aren't buried too deeply.

GERMINATION TEMPERATURES

Heat is something else. Almost all seeds will germinate faster if kept warm, but not too warm. Most seeds will germinate at lower-than-optimum temperatures, but they will take much longer. From seed to harvest, you want plants to grow as quickly as possible; the longer it takes at any stage, the more chance for something bad, such as disease, insects, or drought, to happen.

Seventy-five to 80 degrees is right for most plants, although there are definite exceptions. Published guides say that Solanaceae germinate best at 85 degrees, but all experienced growers know that most varieties of tomatoes don't care much if the soil is somewhat cooler than that. Peppers and eggplant, on the other hand, will germinate very poorly unless that temperature, or nearly that, is constantly maintained until germination. Pansies are said to like alternate heat and cold, which may be why I find them hard to start. The catalog of a good seed company will give the optimum soil temperature for starting each kind of seed. Johnny's is particularly good in this respect.

THE GERMINATION PERIOD

From planting to transplanting is the most difficult time in the life of a plant. It is easier to get a seed to germinate than to keep it alive after it does, although you will find that hard to believe the first time you plant parsley and watch the barren ground for three weeks for any sign of green. (Try pouring water just below boiling temperature on parsley seed twenty-

four hours before planting.) Germinating flats must be kept damp but not wet and warm but not hot.

Keep a cheap thermometer with each flat or group of flats, and try to keep the *soil* temperature above 70 and below 90. A heating tape or other soil-heating system is best. If you don't have one, you might try, at night or on cloudy days, taking the flats out of the greenhouse and putting them on the water heater or refrigerator (where the heat comes out), near but not too near the wood stove or furnace, or over a radiator, register, or portable electric heater. You might be able to heat the whole greenhouse to the desired temperature, but that is a waste and may be bad for other plants.

Fig. 44. Parsley seed can be encouraged to germinate by pouring not-quite-boiling water on it.

In direct sunlight, flats will dry out amazingly fast. You can counteract this by covering them with clear plastic covers or other clear plastic, but watch out! Temperatures under the plastic can go above 100, and the seedlings will be steamed to death. Too cool is bad, but too hot is deadly.

Watch the flats carefully. When the top layer of soil seems totally dry, water them again exactly as you did the first time. *Always* bottom water, never pour water on top of a flat, and *always* use lukewarm water. If the flats are in direct sunlight, you may have to water them more than once a day.

The seeds will germinate in anywhere from five days (zinnias) to a month or more (rosemary). Now you're over the first hurdle. When a sufficient number for your purpose have germinated, you can stop worrying about heat. From now on, they'll do better at about 65 during the day and 55 at night.

Instead, you can start worrying about light. Although it is possible to give mature plants too much light, seedlings should receive as much as you can reasonably provide. Eight to twelve hours is good. If days are very sunny, natural light will be sufficient; if not, you will have to supplement with artificial. Seedlings will lean toward the light, especially on a cloudy day. Rotate the flats to counteract this.

Now you can also worry a bit less about the flat drying out. In fact, when the plants are nearly ready to transplant, it probably won't do any harm if a couple of them wilt from thirst before you water. If they die, they were the weakest ones anyway.

Does that sound like a lot of work? It is. Remember, you're taking care of a baby (more like five hundred babies) from before birth to the toddling stage. Cheer up—baby plants, like most babies, survive in spite of their parents' neglect and abuses. Once you get them into the next stage, you can neglect them a lot more.

DEALING WITH PROBLEMS

Problems arise when you don't want to grow 512 plants all at the same time in the same way, which is pretty much all the time. Some seeds need light, some dark, some heat, some cold. Some take much longer to germinate than others. How do you handle this?

The vast majority of seeds will do well if planted as described above. For special cases, like pansies, you may want to use a separate container in order to keep the seeds cold, or dark, or whatever, although I have planted nemesia, which is said to require dark, in the end rows of a pack, covered the cells with a strip of paper, and gotten good germination.

Some seedlings will be ready to transplant long before others. This is usually not a problem. It is child's play to pop the ones you want out of their cells without disturbing the others. Just continue to keep the remaining ones moist and warm enough.

WHY NOT SIX-PACKS?

Right now you are probably asking yourself, "Why should I go through all this rigmarole? Six-packs are easier to come by and easier to use." Use six-packs if you want to, but I can assure you of this: Once you try the larger containers with tiny cells, you'll never go back.

Let's say you want to start four dozen tomato plants. (Remember, you want to try several different varieties, and you have a lot of friends. If you didn't have them before, you will when they find out you'll furnish them with bedding plants.) You also want to start peppers, herbs, marigolds, and lots of other things, for a total of four hundred. (You'll be surprised how quickly they add up.) Four hundred seedlings will fit very nicely into two 12-by-22-cell flats, which will take up about 3 square feet of bench space. You would need sixty-seven six-packs, taking up 10 square feet, for the same number of plants. Each cell would require about ten times as much soil. Each six-pack would have to be bottom watered. And so on. Try it, if you want to.

Most people who use six-packs or other large-cell containers wind up "saving" time and space by putting more than one seed, usually six or eight, sometimes twelve or more, in a cell. When transplant time comes, the time saved is spent many times over in trying to untangle the root systems of these unfortunate plants. Half or more of them are killed, or at least crippled, in the process. Seed, soil, water, and time are wasted. Where's the saving?

GERMINATION TABLES

Books like this one frequently include a table of germination times, optimum temperatures, and similar "facts." One of the first things a gardener needs to learn is that books, including this one, are frequently wrong or, to put it more politely, that his experience may not be the same as the author's. For example, the first two entries in a germination table in a highly regarded gardening book are "Ageratum, five to eight days; Allysum, four to five days." Another, equally highly regarded, says, "Ageratum, fourteen days; Allysum, ten to twenty days." I find that each takes about ten days, sometimes much longer. There are too many variables. If the medium cools down (for most plants) or dries out, in most cases the sprouting seeds will not be killed; they will just take a lot longer to emerge.

PERSISTENCE

Follow the directions that come with the seeds or are in the catalog, but take them, also, with several grains of salt. Finally, *don't give up!* Parsley is widely regarded as hard to germinate. I don't think it's hard at all, but it takes anywhere from three weeks to two months to show its head. Peppers under optimum conditions will come up in a week to ten days, but I've known them to take a month or more. Almost every greenhouser has had the experience of emptying out the supposedly infertile cell pockets, only to come back a month later to find thyme, peppers, or pansies springing up where he never planted them. Keep the medium moist and warm until the seedlings have germinated or hell has frozen over.

STARTING CUCURBITS

Years ago, nobody started squash and other curcurbits indoors because they, along with a few other vegetables, were considered untransplantable. Market gardeners in northern states changed all that. They found that they could start squash, cucumbers, or melons in the greenhouse, set them out into the garden three or four weeks later, and get a jump on their competitors who were still planting squash seeds in the garden. Now pretty much everybody does this with most cucurbits, although few gardeners or farmers start pumpkins inside.

If you want to start squash or any similarly hard-to-transplant vegetable, flower, or herb in the greenhouse, forget all the advice in this chapter and the next one. Start the seeds three or four weeks before the usual last frost date in your locality, not in small cells but in good-sized pots.

The usual advice is to start them in peat pots and plant them, pot and all, when the time comes. I have had much better luck planting cucurbit seeds in 4-inch round pots. You can also use rectangular containers that are 3 by 4 by 4 inches or thereabouts, but the round ones are easier to slide the plants out of. Use plastic, never clay, for this, unless you are prepared to get the seedlings out by breaking the pot.

Plant about five seeds in each pot, $1/2$ inch deep, in a medium that includes some nourishment. When the true leaves begin to appear, snip off the two or three worst plants at the stem. Don't pull them up, and don't let them live. You may want to select those that leave the rest better spaced. When you start cucurbits inside, you have committed yourself to planting in hills, not rows. The contents of each pot will become a hill.

Move the plants into the garden before they become too large, probably soon after they have three or four true leaves, or earlier if frost is no problem. You can cut apart the pots if you wish, but usually you can remove the plants without damaging them or the pot, if the soil is well dampened. Turn the pot upside down on your left palm with fingers outstretched between the two seedlings. Tap it a few times on the bottom and sides, and remove the pot with your right hand. Quickly turn the contents of your left hand into the hole you have prepared in the garden according to your usual gardening procedures. If you're left-handed, reverse the procedure.

Whether or not frost threatens, it's a great idea to protect cucurbits with floating row covers for the first three or four weeks in the garden. It will not only keep them warmer, but it will also keep pests, particularly striped or spotted cucumber beetles or squash bugs, off them. Remove the covers when the first blossoms appear so the bees can get at them; the bad bugs will never overcome the head start you have given the plants.

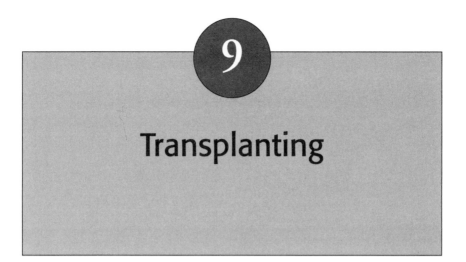

Transplanting

For most parents (there are exceptions), kids become more fun when they begin to walk, maybe even to talk. They still require just as much looking after, maybe more, but they don't seem quite so fragile, and indeed they are not. Plants ready for their first transplanting are much more fun, seem less fragile, but have the advantage over children and puppies that they really don't require as much looking after, partly because they are incapable of locomotion.

SEEDLING NOURISHMENT

As an egg will nourish the baby chick right up to the time it cracks the shell and comes out, a seed contains everything the baby plant needs up to the time when it develops true leaves, and perhaps a little beyond. Adding fertilizer to seed-starting soil is redundant and may do harm, although the swelling seed and beginning plant do need air and water.

DICOTS AND SEED LEAVES

The general rule of thumb is that plants are ready to transplant when they have put forth their first two *true leaves*. This requires a bit of explanation. The first leaf on a seedling is called a *cotyledon,* or *seed leaf.* Most garden plants are dicotyledons, dicots, for short, which means that their cotyledons come as a pair.

As an example of typical dicots, let's take beans; they're large enough and common enough that most gardeners are familiar with how they

Fig. 45. These dicotyledonous plants are showing seed leaves.

sprout. The first leaves, always a pair, and often indistinguishable from the two halves of the bean seed, are seed leaves. Seed leaves are on the plant before it appears above ground.

The next leaves are true leaves. They are very different in appearance from the seed leaves and are similar to what most gardeners think of as typical bean leaves, not surprisingly, because that is what they are.

You will soon learn that all seed leaves look more or less the same. True, squash seed leaves are larger than those of petunias, which you practically need a magnifying glass to see, but they are both smooth sided rather than serrated, plain rather than fancy, and somewhat thicker than the true leaves will be. Seed leaves of tomatoes are long relative to their width and featureless; the next two leaves on the tomato plant, and all the rest forever, will be branched and ferny like all tomato leaves, of whatever variety.

The functions of seed leaves are to contain some nourishment for the baby plant and to get the photosynthesis process started the moment it heaves itself up out of the ground. As soon as the plant gets a good start, they are no longer necessary and start to wither. They sometime hang on a long time after the plant is well started, getting thin and yellow, but eventually they fall off. That's what they're supposed to do.

MONOCOTS

A monocotyledon, or monocot, has only one seed leaf. A typical example is grass. Members of the onion family are about the only monocots raised in the greenhouse. The first leaf of an onion is like a spear. It doesn't appear to be much different from subsequent leaves, which seem to rise straight up out of the first one. The first leaf does die after a while, turning to a sort of brown sheath out of which the next leaf comes.

Monocots also grow very differently from dicots. If you cut off their tips, even when they are very young, they will continue to grow; in fact, it may even benefit them. If you do the same thing to a dicot, it will die, or it may become a useless monster. Sometimes a tomato plant will lose its growing tip as a seedling or won't develop one for some reason. If you don't throw such a plant out, it may live for quite a while, growing thicker, especially at the seed leaves, but not much taller. It will never produce good leaves, blossoms, or fruit.

To clarify your thinking on this subject, consider this: If you mow grass or cut chives, the plant will continue to grow just fine. Try using the lawn mower on beans or tomatoes!

DELAYING TRANSPLANTING

Monocots such as onions may be transplanted at almost any time after the second spear appears. If necessary, transplanting can be delayed quite a while. It can also be delayed with dicots if absolutely necessary; most soil mixes contain enough nutrients to support a seedling for a week or two, although a mix with at least some of your good garden soil is better for this purpose than seed-starting soil mix sold in the store. Sometimes you have to delay, because all seedlings started at the same time don't develop true leaves at the same time. Usually you transplant when the majority are ready; even the ones that have not yet developed true leaves (or don't appear to have; a magnifying glass may tell a different story) will probably do all right.

If it is necessary to delay transplanting for long, you will have to water frequently, perhaps twice a day. The plants are getting too big for their containers and are immediately taking up all the water you give them. Don't think keeping them out of the sunlight will help; that will just make them leggy. Plants that have been delayed will never be as healthy as those transplanted at the right time. Plants that develop long taproots, such as parsley, will be very difficult to transplant if they stay in their original cell too long.

HOW TO TRANSPLANT

If you have followed my advice and started seeds in large flats containing hundreds of tiny cells, transplanting is child's play. All you need is the right-size common nail.

Prepare the containers to receive the transplants just as you prepared the flats for starting seeds, but use a mix that has more garden soil and maybe a little compost or manure. Make sure that the fertilizer is very thoroughly "rotted" or composted—very far from fresh, in other words—and use only a tiny amount. About 5 percent or less of the soil mix might be compost or manure.

Most often the transplants will go into six-packs, but they may go into other containers with larger cells or even into small pots like 4-inchers, especially if they're not going into your garden but will live in your greenhouse or go to a friend. Whatever size you use, bottom water both containers, the present one and the new one, with tepid water. You may have to add more soil mix to the new container and rewater, just as you did when starting seeds.

Fig. 46. Your index finger will make the right-size hole for most transplants.

Approximately in the center of each cell of the new container (if it's a pot, it has only one cell, of course), make a hole with your index finger. You may have to wiggle it around a bit to get the hole large enough to accommodate the plant plus all the soil from the little cell it is coming out of. This is when you will appreciate having used flats with several hundred tiny cells, because the plant along with its soil will fit so nicely into its new home.

Now you need a nail just the right size, something on the order of a 4-penny common. Common nails are the ones with heads. The nail head should fit exactly through the hole in the bottom of the tiny cell, with practically no room to spare. Believe me, nothing works like the right-size nail. If you don't have the kind of house that has a lot of different nails lying around, throw yourself on the mercy of a friend who does, unless you have access to a very old-fashioned hardware store where all the nails are in bins, and you can latch on to one or two of each small size.

Pushing up from underneath with the nail, pop plant and soil out of

Fig. 47. A common nail with a head exactly the right size is the best tool for pushing a seedling out of a tiny cell.

the tiny cell, and coax it into its new location. You should be able to do this by holding it by the moist soil pack and easing it into the hole, tamping some of the soil down around it with the nail head or a finger. If you absolutely have to touch the plant with your fingers, handle it by one or both of the seed leaves, *never* by the stem. Since the seed leaf is going to die soon anyway, even if it tears off it won't do too much damage. In an emergency, handle true leaves before you touch stems or roots.

Fig. 48. The seedling with root ball and soil is encouraged into its new home.

MULTIPLE SEEDLINGS

About the only problem you are likely to encounter—and it is a common one—is when, in the planting process, you inadvertently dropped two or

Fig. 49. It's hard to believe this beautiful petunia plant was once less than an inch long, its roots tangled with those of other petunias.

more seeds into one cell, and you have two petunia or nine chamomile plants where you wanted only one. With some tiny seeds, it's nearly impossible to place just one seed in each cell.

There are three ways to deal with this. The first is to take a pair of cuticle scissors, or some similar tiny snipper, and sever the stem of each plant in the cell except the one that you have decided to let live, the one you think is the best. Don't try to pull out the unwanted ones; you'll injure them all, including the one you want to save. Don't try to pinch them off with your fingernails; the plants are almost always much too small. Do it right away; the longer you wait, the more damage will be done to the best plant.

The second solution is to leave them all, or several, and just carry them through to maturity as a group. This is usually not a good idea, but some plants, like alyssum, will grow just as well and look just as good as a clump. In fact, a few plants look better that way, although this is not the solution for most plants. Peppers and tomatoes, in fact almost all vegetables, will never produce well if they are in a clump.

The last solution is to try to separate the plants and save all, or most. The only way to do this is to immerse the entire bundle in lots and lots of tepid water, and keep teasing them apart with forks, toothpicks, your fingers, or what have you. If, for example, you have a clump of tomatoes, it means, to start with, that you haven't slavishly followed the advice in this book, but it's surprising how successfully you can tease out each individual. If you kill a couple, at least you get to keep the rest. This is the most popular solution; the first one is the best.

Don't try to save crippled plants. They will never do well for you, and they'll take a lot of time you need to spend on the best specimens. These aren't human beings, or even puppies. Destroy any that are not growing as well as the others.

USING A SPRAY

When transplanting, keep a garden sprayer handy, filled with tepid water. Set it just above the finest setting, and adjust it to suit your needs. Sometimes you can coax a seedling down into a hole in its new location with a spray or fine jet, making it unnecessary to touch it with your fingers. A strong spray is often helpful in separating seedlings tangled together; sometimes it's the only way.

CLEANSING

Newly transplanted seedlings often, or almost always, have tiny crumbs of soil on their leaves. These should be cleaned off, if possible, using a very fine spray of tepid water. Try to end with the seedling upright; a plant with one leaf in the mud is going to suffer a considerable setback. Sometimes you can hold the tiny plant up with one finger while spraying on the opposite side.

Try to give newly transplanted seedlings enough light and warmth to bring them along and especially to dry the leaves after cleansing them, but don't expose them to many hours of strong sunlight and high heat right after they are transplanted. If possible, transplant early on a day when sun is forecast, so that the greenhouse will be warm and bright, and put the new transplants in a warm, bright, but not sunny spot. By the following day, they should be ready for a few hours of sun.

SUBSEQUENT TRANSPLANTINGS

Occasionally you will need to transplant a second time, or even more. Sometimes this will be because you started seedlings for the garden too soon and need to hold them in the greenhouse longer. If this happens, don't try to keep them too long in small flats or pots; they will never be as healthy later. Keep them as dry, cool, and brightly lit as you dare, but when they are clearly outgrowing their containers, if you can't yet put them outdoors, transplant them again.

The other case in which you will be transplanting more than once will occur with houseplants or crop plants that are never going outdoors. This process is arbitrarily called "potting on" rather than "transplanting" and is discussed in chapter 11.

CARE OF TRANSPLANTS

Transplants remaining in the greenhouse need no special care; in fact, they are a good deal less work than new seedlings. Water them when they seem dry, give them all the sun possible, and feed them with a dilute solution of fish emulsion or manure tea, but only if they have been in the greenhouse more than two weeks since they were transplanted. Begin as soon as possible to harden them off.

Hardening Off
and Setting Out

If the plants you grow in your greenhouse will never leave the premises—that is, if they are all houseplants or vegetables or flowers you are growing for harvest indoors—you can skip this chapter. You are also a member of a very small group. Most greenhousers, somewhere around 99 and $^{44}/100$ percent of us, use their greenhouses predominantly or exclusively for starting seeds and raising seedlings to be sold, given away, or most commonly, set out in their gardens.

If one or more of these three is the ultimate destination of your plants, they should be hardened off. If you are going to place them in your own garden, or if you are going to furnish them to others free or for cash or in exchange for their plants, you should have information on how to set them out, for yourself and to pass on to your clients. Never give or sell a plant to a beginning gardener without a few words of advice on storage and planting; I once had someone leave tomato plants outdoors on a frosty night and complain that they had all died. You may already know a good deal about setting out and something about hardening off, but a refresher course won't hurt.

HARDENING OFF

Before they leave the protected environment of the greenhouse for the great outdoors, plants must be hardened off. If you skip this step, your plants may die in the garden; at best, they will sit there much longer before they perk up and take hold.

You begin the hardening-off process as soon as the seedlings appear. Most seeds germinate best at a higher temperature than that which is optimum for their growth after germination. Tomatoes, for example, germinate best at about 85 degrees but should be kept at about 65 after the seeds have germinated. Seeds should always be kept moist, but most seedlings may be allowed to dry out between waterings. It may be hard for you to control the temperature of your greenhouse exactly, but you can certainly control watering.

After a few weeks of that program, harden off plants further by putting them out on a porch or deck. Later, put them right outdoors. Start them with half an hour on a very mild day; work them up to half a day in the sun and wind when the outdoor temperature is about 55 or higher, always bearing in mind that some plants, such as cabbages, like cold weather and others, such as peppers, don't.

The hardening-off process is by no means only to accustom the plants to colder temperatures. It is also to accustom them to other rigors of outdoor life, such as wind, sun, and drought. Sunlight outside the greenhouse is much stronger than inside. Watch them closely; if there is the slightest sign of wilting, don't sprinkle them with the hose; bring them back into the greenhouse and bottom water them. A few days later, you might bottom water them right out on the deck.

Wind is also very dangerous. Plants can get too dry very quickly on a sunny day with low humidity and wind, and wind can also break tall stems. You can actually do your plants a great deal of good if, long before the outdoor hardening-off process begins, you brush your hand lightly over all of them occasionally. There have been scientific studies that show that plants treated thus are healthier than those left alone. Presumably, stems and branches strengthen in response to this stimulus.

Drying Out

As time goes on and the seedlings grow stronger, let more time elapse between waterings, allowing them to dry out thoroughly. Watch them carefully; if they wilt, revive them. It's worth noting that the two periods during which greenhouse plants must be watched constantly are when they are very small and when they are about to be set out; between these times, benign neglect is in order.

Fig. 50. A deck just the right height outside the greenhouse door is the perfect place for hardening off your plants. Place them on a cart and simply wheel them in and out as necessary.

Cold Treatment

According to some growers, peppers and tomatoes will produce better if, after the first transplant, plants experience nighttime temperatures in the greenhouse of about 55 degrees for three or four weeks. Then they should again be exposed to nighttime temperatures of about 70. This technique, or a similar one, might work on other plants, such as eggplant, but most hobby greenhouse owners don't have the ability to control temperatures to that degree, especially when there are other plants in the greenhouse that require more usual conditions.

Setting Out

If plants have been raised correctly up to this point and hardened off properly, there is nothing very tricky about setting them out. Get each pot or flat and its contents thoroughly wet. At this stage, as with previous transplantings, there is no such thing as too wet. (Market gardeners refer to setting out lettuce as "mudding in" and give the job to the worker with the least seniority.) Dig a hole in the garden about twice the size of the pot or cell. Make sure the soil is loosened several inches *below* where the plant will rest. In most cases, it is better not to put compost or manure directly in the hole, but rather to have rich soil everywhere in the garden. Squash and other cucurbits are an exception to this rule, but if you use chemical fertilizers, never let any come in direct contact with roots or leaves.

Fill the hole about halfway with water. Carefully pop the plant and its wet ball of roots out of the pot or flat and into the hole. If the plant is alone in a pot, follow directions for cucurbits in the preceding chapter. If it is in a six-pack or similar container, press on the bottom of the cell with your thumb and catch the emerging plant with the other hand. If this injures the flat, so be it.

If the plant is particularly sensitive to damaged roots, carefully crack and break apart the pot and throw it away. Use garden scissors or tin snips if necessary. The plant will never know it has been transplanted. This is the procedure often used with all cucurbits and with other plants that are generally regarded as hard to transplant, such as parsley. Pots are very easy to come by; you don't want to lose a zinnia that you have lovingly tended for a month, and you certainly don't want to lose the jump on the season that you get from starting such plants indoors.

PREVENTING WILTING

Many plants wilt in the sun when they are first set out. Curiously, this has little to do with their overall hardiness. Lettuce and brassicas are great wilters, tomatoes and peppers less so. The cold hardiness of these plants is inversely proportional to their likeliness to wilt—that is, lettuce and cabbages will stand a lot of cold but wilt easily, whereas tomatoes and peppers die at the first sign of frost but are much less likely to wilt when first set out in the garden.

Wilting won't kill the plants, or even hurt them much, directly, but it can cause indirect damage. It slows them down and makes them vulnerable to insects and disease. Lettuce that seemed to be at death's door the first week it was set out will produce fine heads and leaves in a month or two.

Wilt can be prevented or lessened to some degree by the care taken to protect roots and by thorough watering in. Needless to say, thorough watering should continue for several days to a week if nature does not provide moisture.

Note: The term *wilt* here refers to the temporary drooping of a plant's leaves. The term is also applied to a disease that produces similar symptoms but is more serious and long-lasting, and may eventually kill the plant.

Covering

Wilt can also be prevented by protecting plants from the sun for the first few days. Cover them with floating row covers, store-bought plastic or paper cloches or "hot caps," plastic gallon jugs with the bottoms cut off, or something similar.

One of the best covers would seem to be the pot they came out of. Unfortunately, you almost always need the next size larger. In a pinch, prop large pieces of cardboard against stakes to shade plants from sunlight; such shade may have to be moved, but if it is large enough and to the south, it will probably do. Wind will wreak havoc with your shade arrangement; be careful that it doesn't drop the protecting device on the infant plant and smash it. Pots that shade plants should be held down with large stones.

Fig. 51. The tops of plastic jugs make good protective covers for newly transplanted plants.

It is not heat so much as light that makes plants wilt; if it drizzles for three days after you set them out, you've got it made. It is rather a nuisance, but the best practice is to take the covers off every morning for an hour or two, then cover them all day, uncover them for several hours at dusk, then cover them for the night, unless it's going to be a warm one. Obviously, this schedule is impractical if you're using floating row covers.

Pruning

Another cause of wilt is the loss of roots in the setting-out procedure. Plants have a mechanism that protects roots by moving water from the leaves to the roots if they are stressed. Your plants will be healthier if you prune off a few leaves to counterbalance this loss. Many older books advise both root pruning and leaf pruning, especially with monocots such as leeks and onions. I have experimented with leeks, and have never found any advantage to this practice.

WHEN TO SET OUT

The best weather for setting out plants is a cool, but not cold, drizzle. The air temperature should be in the high 50s or low 60s. In a pinch, it can be cooler or slightly warmer. If a drizzle is not available, set out late in the day, so that the plants will have late-afternoon shade and overnight to adapt to their new surroundings.

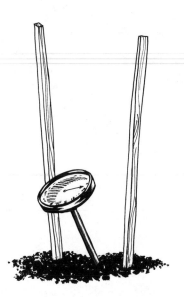

In deciding when to set out plants, soil temperature is more important than air temperature, and a soil thermometer is a must. Leave it in the ground for several days, and read it two or three times a day. You will be surprised how much it varies. Mark its location with several tall sticks; otherwise, you will step on it or run over it with the garden tractor.

Some gardeners, maybe most, take pleasure in being the first on the block to have peas, tomatoes, or what have you. It is a good deal wiser to have more and healthier tomatoes rather than earlier ones; usually they're only about a week later. Of the Solanaceae, tomatoes are tender, peppers tenderer, eggplant tenderest. Tomatoes set out much before June 1 (in Zone 4) don't die; they just sit there. Tomatoes set out two weeks later will soon catch up with, and frequently surpass, those set out earlier.

Fig. 52. A soil thermometer in the garden is likely to get stepped on or run over; the sticks make its presence more obvious.

Peppers that experience a night below 40 degrees, even though there is no frost, may drop buds. A month later they will have lovely foliage but no fruit.

A rule of thumb for setting out is that plants that can stand a lot of fall cold, like cabbages, can be set out earlier in the spring. One organic market gardener starts Brussels sprouts in March, not in the greenhouse, but outdoors. Plants that turn black with the slightest touch of frost, like basil, should not be set out until the soil is thoroughly warmed, with nighttime soil temperatures not dipping below 60.

FLOWERS

The guidelines above apply about equally to flowers as to vegetables or herbs. Biennials or perennials, such as delphiniums, foxgloves, columbines, and pansies, can be set out quite early. (Pansies are biennials or perennials in mild climates; where we live they sometimes winter over, especially if mulched, sometimes not. They also self-sow, so it's sometimes hard to tell.) Hardy annuals can be set out after the soil has reached 55 or so; tender annuals have to wait longer. Most common garden flowers don't seem to wilt when first set out, but covering them as described above can't hurt.

Fig. 53. Foxglove.

Fig. 54. Pansy.

PART III

Houseplants

General Information about Houseplants

Webster's defines *houseplant* as "a plant grown or kept indoors." That doesn't work very well for our purposes. I start basil indoors and keep it indoors in the wintertime, but I don't consider it a houseplant. Probably you don't either. Let's say that a houseplant is one grown primarily indoors, although it may be placed outside temporarily in warm weather, in a pot. It is grown for its appearance rather than for culinary purposes or as a source of cut blooms. In other words, neither parsley in a pot on a kitchen window nor zinnias in a bed in the greenhouse are houseplants by this definition.

For some reason, many persons who grow plants indoors quickly cease to be generalists and become specialists in some kind of houseplant. There are orchid fanciers, African violet growers, gardeners who love and tend cacti or bromeliads, and many others. It is impossible for this book to give more than a cursory treatment to any one kind of plant, partly because the author is fairly ignorant about many plants that specialists love, such as orchids, African violets, and cacti. Anyone who becomes seriously interested in one of these specialties can find dozens, if not hundreds, of books just on that subject.

HISTORY

People didn't bring plants into the house much in earlier times, at least not in the United States. There were obvious reasons. Most people had to work so long and hard that they didn't have time for frills. Most houses, except for the area close to the fireplace, weren't conspicuously warmer than outdoors, and houses were dark, even in the daytime, with only a few small windows, often "glazed" with something like oiled paper.

In the nineteenth century, however, especially in the latter half, houseplants became very popular. They throve in the steam-heated houses and apartments of that era. Most people can remember Grandmother's house, filled with ferns and ivies.

There are as many fads and trends in gardening as in any other activity. What Grandmother loved may now be out of fashion, although it may still be pleasant and charming to grow, even though the gardening faddists will look down their noses at you. There are also trends in the names of plants and even their pronunciation. What you call wandering Jew (*Tradescantia fluminensis*), a name now considered politically incorrect, someone else may call spiderwort. A third person may use the term wandering Jew for a different but related plant, *Zebrina pendula*. For this reason, and not because they are pedantic, authors often include Latin names for plants.

CONDITIONS

As surprising as it may sound, the greenhouse is often not the best place to keep houseplants. At least in northern climes, almost no noncommercial grower keeps houseplants in a freestanding greenhouse; it's too cold in winter and too hot in summer. (Every time I write a line like that, I know I'll get a letter from the irate exception that proves the rule.)

Many of the most popular houseplants, especially the older ones, like a Boston fern, were selected because they would thrive in the dry, overheated, relatively dark conditions of a city home. Move one of these to the sunlit, humid, and often cooler conditions of a home greenhouse, and it may die, or at least not do well.

There are many houseplants that can be grown in a typical attached greenhouse and many others that can be grown in some room in the house other than the greenhouse, a room that is warmer, or drier, or has more subdued and diffuse light than the greenhouse. It is often convenient and practical to start such plants in the greenhouse or to take them back there for watering or other treatment. It is almost always easier and neater to take them to the potting bench in the greenhouse for repotting. Bear in mind, however, that some houseplants, especially those that have grown almost to the size of trees, become acclimated to a certain location and very much resent being moved around. Ficus is a notable example.

Don't make the mistake of thinking that you can grow all sorts of different houseplants in the same greenhouse or in the same room in the house. It just can't be done. It is possible that you have a warm, humid greenhouse (or even laundry room) where certain sorts of plants will thrive, if you can provide them with the proper light conditions, and a cool, dry room in another part of the house where other plants will do well, but cacti and African violets are never going to thrive cheek by jowl. They may not die, but at least one of them will not be doing as well as it could.

Many plants can adapt to less-than-ideal conditions if the change comes slowly. That's why plants to be set out in the garden go through a hardening-off process. Plants brought in from the garden, as well as plants moved from one environment to another that is quite different, should go through an acclimatization process. Bring plants from the garden to a deck or porch for a week or two before moving them into the house. In the same way, if you want to move a plant from a shady to a sunny or a humid to a dry indoor location, do it gradually if possible.

KINDS OF HOUSEPLANTS
Most people are willing to grant that snapdragons and cosmos, morning glories and zinnias are beautiful, although gardeners may differ over which they prefer. For some odd reason, many, possibly most, houseplants are ugly. I hasten to say that by that I mean that their beauty is sometimes hidden from the layman. With regard to houseplants, beauty is most certainly in the eye of the beholder. I don't find aloes pretty, although they are useful, and many popular houseplants, such as kalanchoes, seem to me more bizarre than beautiful. There are, however, cactus lovers who would hug the spiny creatures to their bosoms if there were not practical drawbacks to this procedure. Don't knock somebody else's spider plant, and he may not criticize your Swedish ivy.

Many more houseplants are grown for the beauty and interest of their foliage than for their blooms. Partly this is because plants that thrive in typical house conditions generally fall into two groups: jungle (rain forest) plants and desert plants.

Jungle Plants
Contrary to what we might think, the jungle, at least the understory (the part on or near the ground, below the overspreading canopy of trees), is

not a place of bright sunlight, but of diffuse light. Plants that originated here can easily make do with the light inside a house, if they get enough moisture.

Often the houseplant grower can produce a miniclimate more humid than the rest of the house. A group of potted plants growing in close proximity to each other, if they are kept sufficiently watered, will have air surrounding them that is moister than the air 10 feet away. This effect can be enhanced by physically misting the plants.

It is usually not beneficial to have a potted plant sitting in a saucer of water, but it is useful to have several of them all placed on a bed of coarse gravel that is kept damp. High-humidity plants also benefit from an occasional shower. Put them in the tub and treat them to a warm, gentle rain for a few minutes. Then let them drain for at least half an hour before returning them to their usual location.

Desert Plants: Cacti and Succulents

Plants that originated in the desert or other dry areas are readily adaptable to the dry conditions of the home. They need infrequent but thorough watering, and they need to drain very thoroughly after a watering. Aloes and jade plants can go a month or more without watering, if they are kept out of direct sunlight. On the other hand, some varieties of cacti may benefit from watering as frequently as once a week, if they are getting a lot of sunlight. You need to be aware of how many successive cloudless days have passed.

"FLOWERING" AND "NONFLOWERING" PLANTS

Of course, all plants flower—that is, all but primitive plants like ferns, which produce spores but can't be said to flower in the usual sense. Some houseplants are believed by their owners never to flower; this may be true, as in the case of ferns, or the blooms may be so odd or so inconspicuous as not to be recognized, or the plant simply may not flower under the conditions in which it is kept.

Many owners of jade plants, for example, keep them out of direct sunlight. There is nothing wrong with this procedure, but if the plants are moved outdoors for the summer, several things will happen. First, the leaves will acquire a reddish hue, especially on the edges, that the owner may or may not find attractive. Much later, often after the plants have been brought back inside, they may break out in very attractive small, white, star-shaped blooms. This usually happens only with older jade plants.

The next two chapters divide houseplants into "flowering" and "nonflowering" categories. Most of the plants categorized as "nonflowering" actually do bloom, but they are kept because of the beauty or interest of their foliage, not of their blooms. A few never bloom; others, like *Monstera deliciosa,* don't bloom in the light, heat, and moisture conditions under which they are usually kept.

COMMERCIAL "HOUSEPLANTS"

Huge hotels and malls are using plants more and more in their atria and other rooms. Many of these "houseplants" are trees and shrubs, some of them two stories high. Commercial establishments find that plants act as air fresheners and diminish indoor air pollution. The plants, together with the care they must be given, reduce the dryness of the indoor atmosphere. Many of these establishments use fans to keep air circulating gently indoors, which not only improves air quality but also keeps plants healthier. An expert in caring for plants in hotels and similar establishments offers the following suggestions, most of which can be used by hobby gardeners.

You may not be able to use fans to stimulate your plants, but brush them gently with your sleeve or hand as you walk past; it will strengthen stems.

Water infrequently and thoroughly with tepid water, from the bottom if possible. Buy an inexpensive soil moisture tester to be sure soil isn't too damp, or stick your finger well down in the pot to see if the soil has dried out. If leaf tips turn black, that may be a sign of overwatering; if they turn brown, underwatering.

Plants that touch glass may get sunburn or frostbite, even if the glass is double. Leave an inch of space between leaves and glass, and remember that plants grow.

With regard to pests, a dormant oil preparation called Sunspray is designed specifically for houseplants and is particularly effective against whitefly. This expert also suggests that the houseplant owner should not wait for signs of insects but should spray routinely with a soap solution or use rubbing alcohol in a mister as a preventive measure. And here's an unusual idea: Tabasco sauce around the base of a huge plant will discourage ants.

SOILS AND FERTILIZERS

The information on soils, water, air, diseases, and pests given in other chapters applies as well to houseplants as to greenhouse growing, with certain additions or subtractions. In the greenhouse, and certainly in the garden, you probably won't find the smell of fish emulsion or manure tea too offensive. In the house, especially if you have housemates, you may have to use liquid chemical fertilizer specifically designed for houseplants or particular species. At least you can try the organic fertilizers first.

In the two chapters that follow, you will frequently read something like "Give them a feeding of half-strength liquid houseplant fertilizer every other week." If you add compost or manure to the soil when potting, this may not be necessary, at least in the first year. Be sure the material is totally dry and composted, and mix it thoroughly with the soil, or put some of it at the bottom of the pot, where the plants roots will not touch it immediately. Most indoor plants have a period when they are relatively dormant and a period when they send out new shoots and leaves. The latter is when the plant needs additional feeding.

Many houseplants need special soil mixtures. These are so varied that they are discussed under specific plants in the next chapters, as are water, humidity, light, and temperature requirements. In some cases, the best thing you can do is buy African violet soil or begonia soil at the garden supply store.

PROPAGATION OTHER THAN FROM SEEDS

Almost all plants raised to be transplanted outdoors are started from seeds. Many, if not most, houseplants are propagated in other ways. These include dividing and making leaf or stem cuttings.

In some cases, alternative propagation may be a fad. Geraniums are almost never grown from seed but can be easily, and there are some advantages in doing so. It may be heresy, but if you are considering raising a certain houseplant, such as a coleus or gloxinia, you might be wisest to buy one from a florist. This will give you a chance to learn what care it needs and how much you enjoy it before you go to a great deal of trouble over its propagation.

Dividing

Most houseplants that can be propagated by division do it for you, many so prolifically as to become a nuisance. If you are familiar with spider plants, you know what I mean. These produce "babies" at the ends of runners (underground runners are *stolons*). Stick the baby in a pot, whether or not it has already rooted somewhere else. When it takes hold, cut the runner. Then try to find someone to adopt the baby.

Aloes, jade plants, and many other plants are equally easy. Jade plants, like many other houseplants, put out *air roots*. These are roots that form on a branch and hang down in air. Sometimes, as on Swiss cheese plants, they grow 3 feet or longer. In the wild, eventually they reach the ground; in houses, seldom. Jade plants, after a while, drop babies that have these roots. In our greenhouse, some fall in the pot, some on the slate floor. I have picked them up off the floor a week or two later and stuck them in a pot, where they flourished.

A pot containing an aloe will sooner or later have baby plants peeking out the drain holes. If you let them go too long, you'll have to kill the off-spring plant or break the pot. Other babies grow from the main plant beside it in the pot. If you take them out of the pot, tearing the two apart is easy, and each will grow. Other dividable plants may have to be pulled apart with strong fingers or two forks (garden, not kitchen). A last resort is to use a sharp knife, but this technique is the most likely to injure both halves and let disease in.

Cuttings

There is considerable furor right now over cloning. What's the fuss? Gardeners have been cloning plants for years. About as soon as people started growing plants indoors, they began doing what our grandmothers called *slipping*. Some plants adapt to this with ridiculous ease. Like most gardeners, I prune tomato vines by pulling out the suckers that come up in what I call the "upside-down armpits" of the plant—that is, between the main stem and a legitimate branch. Sometimes I slip the suckers, by poking a hole in the garden dirt near the mother plant and sticking the sucker in it. That's all. Much more than half the time, the slip takes root and eventually produces tomatoes.

Some plants are harder to slip; some verge on the impossible. Geraniums are typically easy. Here's how to slip a geranium or similar plant. First, prepare a propagation case, which is a box with a clear plastic cover. Friends will give you these, you can make them, or you can buy one. Fill it with sand, peat moss, vermiculite, or a mixture of these. I prefer sand.

Growers refer to sand used in the greenhouse as "sharp sand" or "builders' sand," but about the only kinds that won't work are beach sand or sand your highway department uses in winter, because they're both salty.

Thoroughly moisten the medium, and keep it that way. Take a 4-to-6-inch stem cutting from a fairly new green shoot, not a woody part. Remove any blossoms or buds and most leaves, especially large ones, but leave two or three. Dip the end for about an inch into a hormonal root cutting powder, such as Rootone. (I find many of the less difficult plants root as well without this, but it couldn't hurt and it doesn't cost much.)

Make a hole in the propagation bed with an appropriate-size finger or pencil, and stick the cutting in the hole. The rooting powder, if any, shouldn't show above the sand, but about two-thirds of the cutting should. Don't ram the stem in hard enough to injure it, but be sure there isn't any air space

Fig. 55. A geranium stem tip that has been prepared for slipping.

under it. Put a dozen or two cuttings in a case. Don't let the cover touch the plants or one plant touch another. If you use a homemade cover made of thin plastic, prop it up with lollipop sticks or something similar.

Now go away for a month or so, but be sure the medium stays moist. Keep the case warm all the time, but not in direct sun. This usually means putting artificial heat under it. When new leaf growth starts, pull the cutting out gently (that's why I like sand better than peat) and inspect it. If there is much discernible root, pot it up. If not, replace it carefully and wait some more. If you're lucky, about half the slips will root eventually. The other half will finally rot, which means it's time to throw them away.

Your grandmother may have just stuck slips in a glass of water on a windowsill. This works fairly well with easy plants and has the merit that you can tell at a glance if roots are emerging. A slight refinement is to cover the top of the glass with aluminum foil with a hole in it just large enough to admit the slip. If you use this method, skip the hormonal powder.

Advanced students who grow things like African violets do leaf petiole cuttings or leaf cuttings. A *petiole* is a leaf stem; you've seen millions. Pull a leaf, with petiole, off the plant and follow the directions above, with these exceptions: Make the hole, with a pencil or lollipop stick, at an angle, and put the leaf in it face up. Don't pull it up to look for roots; baby plants will appear at the base of the leaf. You put it in at an angle right side up so that they won't be shaded or concealed by the mother leaf.

Fig. 56. A kalanchoe shoot thathas put forth roots in a glass of water.

Many call this procedure taking a leaf cutting, but in the true leaf cutting process, a leaf is torn along its center vein, and half, or even less, inserted a short distance into the propagation case. Baby plants, sometimes a great number, appear in due time. They may have to be carefully teased apart.

Fig. 57. A propagation case filled with leaf petiole cuttings; it will have a clear plastic cover.

Air Layering

Air layering sounds a great deal harder than it really is. It is a method for producing more dieffenbachia or rubber plants and for counteracting the tendency these plants have to become unsightly by dropping all their leaves except those at the very top, presenting a long expanse of thick, not very attractive stem.

To propagate in this way, cut a slit in the stem diagonally upward with a sharp knife. It's a good idea to sterilize the knife first. Prop the slit open with a toothpick or wooden match, and dust the opening with hormonal rooting powder. Bandage the wound, toothpick and all, with wet sphagnum peat moss, extending it all the way around the stem. Cover this with clear plastic, tying it on. In a few months (this technique is not for the impatient), roots will start to thread their way out through the moss. Remove the plastic, cut the stem off below the slit, and plant the new plant with the old top.

Fig. 58. The first step in air layering: slitting the stem and holding the slit open with a toothpick.

You can cut one or more lengths from the bare stem or cane that is now sticking up in the air and propagate them in a case. Lay them in horizontally, push them into the moist sand about halfway, and in a while tiny new plants will appear at the edges. Remove these by cutting a chunk out of the cane around them, and plant. With some plants, like Swiss cheese plant, you can cut the original plant back to the base, and even it will spring up again.

Fig. 59. The second step in air layering: covering the wound with damp sphagnum peat moss.

POTTING ON

Houseplant growers speak of "potting up" and "potting on." The first means putting a plant in a pot; the second means taking it out of that pot and putting it in a bigger pot. Both are similar to the transplanting procedure in chapter 9, but there is this difference: Plants you grow to be moved into the garden will not live in pots very long; those that are houseplants will live in them forever.

Plants in pots eventually become pot-bound—that is, they outgrow their pots. Plants vary, but in most cases it is a mistake to pot on before this stage is reached. In fact, some flowering plants bloom much more profusely if they are pot-bound. There are several ways to tell when a plant is pot-bound. Because the pot is full of roots, with relatively little soil, water added at the top will run right down the side, inside, and immediately come out the drainage hole. If you turn the pot upside down, the plant, including the root mass, will slide out very easily. Finally, roots will begin to crawl out the drainage hole or holes. If the pot has the tiniest crack, the roots will find it and slither through.

Try to pot on in late winter or early spring, just before or as the plant begins a growth spurt. Don't put a little plant in a big pot to save trouble later; it won't do as well. Go up just one or two sizes. In other words, move a plant from a 4-inch pot to a 6-inch pot.

Prepare first. Be sure there is plenty of drainage material at the bottom of the pot. Clay-pot fanciers always use broken pot material for this; they always have plenty of it around. I use gravel or small stones that I have screened out of my garden soil.

Put an inch or two of the desired soil mix in the bottom of the pot. Don't put in much; there won't be room for the transplantee. Turn the pot upside down and tap it once or twice. Catch the plant with two spread fingers as it emerges. If it won't come out readily, even after you add plenty of water, roots are probably caught in cracks. In that case, destroy the pot, taking care not to injure the plant; it's much more valuable to you than the pot. Place the plant in its new home, push it down gently, and add soil around it with one hand while holding it in place with the other. Tamp down firmly. That's it.

That's it, except that, since many plants grow forever if unchecked, you may someday have to move a "tree" that weighs 150 pounds from a 30-inch pot to a 36-incher. Good luck. You may decide that it can just stay pot-bound, or you may lay the young tree as carefully as possible on the greenhouse floor and pull the pot off it, then try to get it into its new pot. Fortunately, even quite small plants are more rugged than you think, and it's hard to kill a small tree with this kind of handling, if you keep it moist enough afterward.

Finally, don't be intimidated out of acquiring a certain kind of houseplant because the directions for care seem difficult and complicated. The directions for growing tomatoes in the outdoor garden seem complicated to someone who has never done it—fertilizing, watering if necessary, providing enough sun, pruning, staking. You quickly got the hang of it, and even something like air layering is not nearly so difficult as it sounds.

Remember, too, that plants are a lot tougher than we think. If you don't give a philodendron exactly the recommended conditions, it may not win a prize at the philodendron show, but it will still provide your home or greenhouse with beauty and charm.

Some plants really do demand precision and skill in care and handling. That's why you won't find orchids covered in this book. If you have a yen to try your hand at growing orchids, however, don't be dissuaded. Buy a plant at the florist, get all the information you can, and go to it. After all, what's the worst thing that can happen?

Flowering Houseplants

There are thousands of kinds of flowering plants that are grown indoors, and each kind comes in many varieties. Listed below are a few of the most popular. Some are most popular with plant lovers in general; a few sneaked in because they are most popular with me. Unlike foliage plants, flowering houseplants require such a wide variety of moisture, light, soil, and nutrient conditions that no general rules can be stated here.

Note: Whenever I suggest that houseplants be put outdoors in the summer, I mean in a pot, not out of it, and in a semisheltered location such as a porch or deck. Exceptions will be noted.

AFRICAN VIOLET (*Saintpaulia***)**
A friend of mine pronounces the common name of *Saintpaulia* "friggin violet," because he finds African violets hard to grow, but they wouldn't be so popular if they were *that* difficult. Treated right, they will bloom all year round, although they will have periods of less bloom followed by explosions of color. Originally violet (surprise!), they now come in practically any color and many sizes. They

Fig. 60. African violet.

are usually grown from leaf petiole cuttings but can be started from seed.

Proper treatment for African violets consists of not too much of anything—light, water, humidity, or fertilizer—but just enough. In addition, they will suffer if nights are too cool. These qualities make them better houseplants than greenhouse plants. African violet soil can never be allowed to dry out. They should be bottom watered and can be sprayed but not misted. (This is generally true of fuzzy-leaved plants.) Many enthusiasts grow them exclusively under artificial light, since they like bright light but not direct sun. If all this sounds like your cup of tea, you will soon be entering your fancy variegated double *Saintpaulias* in shows.

BEGONIA (*Begonia*)

There are several different kinds of begonias, and each requires a slightly different kind of care. Tuberous begonias produce spectacular blossoms of many colors and types. Most gardeners that grow these outdoors in a shady location simply dig up the tubers in late summer, store them over the winter, and plant them again in late spring. In essence, you can do this in a cool greenhouse, but you can start them in early March or perhaps have them continue blooming later in the fall. You can buy plants or start them from cuttings, tubers, or seed.

Wax begonias are of the same family and are less showy but more reliable, in the sense that they bloom all year long. They can be grown from seed or stem cuttings, fairly easily in both cases.

Both types of begonias like nights well below 60 degrees. Both can be set outside in summer; wax begonias, contrary to popular belief, will flourish in full sun, whereas tuberous will not. Tuberous begonias like much more humid conditions than their cousins. They should be kept moist at all times; wax need to be watered thoroughly but allowed to dry out between waterings. Both can be fed with dilute liquid fertilizer twice a month.

CAMELLIA (*Camellia*)

Camellias are very elegant flowers, reminiscent of the frail ladies of the nineteenth century and unrequited love. You can propagate them from stem cuttings, a difficult but not impossible process, or you can simply buy a plant. They like bright light but not direct sun, fairly acid soil with some humus, not too much water, and cool temperatures, especially during the period of bloom, when temperatures should be about 50 at night and 65 in the daytime.

There are many, many varieties, a few of which are wonderfully fragrant. Like many flowering houseplants, they can be put outdoors in summer, in light shade. Most bloom for about six weeks, but by careful selection of varieties, you can have them in bloom from October to April. Colors range from white through pink to red.

CAPE PRIMROSE (*Streptocarpus*)

The Latin name of this plant, which many use, sounds like a disease, which may be the reason why this African violet relative, which for my money is prettier, more interesting, and easier to grow than its better-known cousin, is not more popular.

Some varieties can be started from seed; others are started from stem, leaf petiole, or actual leaf cuttings.

All need essentially the same care as African violets since, as their names suggest, both these plants originated in tropical South African jungles, but Cape primroses are less delicate than African violets. Originally all were blue; now there are pinks and other colors. Roughly petunia-shaped blooms are at the ends of long spikes, providing a beautiful and intriguing display.

Fig. 61. Cape primrose.

CYCLAMEN (*Cyclamen*)

Cyclamen persicum is a lovely houseplant that grows from a corm, a structure something like a bulb. Other cyclamens occur in the wild; they are less showy and much less frequently grown as houseplants. Probably the best way to start is to buy a *C. persicum* in the fall and watch its growth cycle. It will have dozens of butterflylike buds that arise as the earlier blossoms die and you pull them off. Eventually it will be reduced to a bare corm, or one with a small amount of old foliage. Either way, give it a period of dormancy, start watering again in June, and the plant will begin its cycle again. Don't prolong the period of dormancy; I put one in a corner of the cellar and forgot it for two years. Somewhat to my surprise, I couldn't coax it back to life.

More than any other plant, cyclamen must be bottom watered. If the top area of the corm, under the foliage, stays wet, corm and foliage will rot. The corm should protrude above the soil line; the older the plant, the more this is true. Cyclamens like bright sun, direct or indirect, and a good deal of water when blooming. Gradually decrease the water as the cycle is drawing to a close, and provide more shade. It can be put out in a shady spot in summer, but don't let it get too wet.

These plants are among many that like it quite cool; if it experiences nighttime temperatures much above 50 during the period of bloom, it won't die, but it won't do well. Cyclamens can be grown from seed, but it is difficult. After planting, keep the seeds in total darkness for more than a month, don't let them dry out, and check every day toward the end of that period.

EASTER CACTUS (*Rhipsalidopsis gaertneri*)
There are Easter cacti, Christmas cacti, and even Thanksgiving cacti. They are similar but not identical and will bloom at the time specified if handled correctly. The Easter cactus has bright red flowers; the "leaves" are hard to describe. As anyone who has ever seen one knows, with these plants, the "leaves" are also the "stem." The Easter cactus thrives at house temperatures, but curiously for a cactus, it likes to live in bright shade in moist soil.

Usually the gardener will buy or be given one, it will bloom on or near the correct date and then will never function properly again.

Fig. 62. Easter cactus.

To avoid this, when it stops blooming, continue to give it the same care you gave it previously. You can set it outdoors, in shade, over the summer.

It will go into a dormant phase in early September and will bloom again *if* it is given *either* nights down to 50 degrees *or* the same kind of pitch-dark treatment given poinsettias. An easy way out is this: If it is left out until just before the first frost, it will probably have had cool enough nights. But don't let frost touch it; that will be the end of it. During the dormant period, it should have minimal water and no fertilizer. If you want to give your friends Easter cacti, you can propagate them without too much difficulty from a short piece of stem tip.

EASTER LILY (*Lilium longiflorum*)
The Latin name of Easter lily means "long-flowering lily." You can get the gift plant you received at Easter to bloom again if you handle it right. It probably won't bloom precisely at Easter, but it will bloom. Easter is, after all, a movable feast.

While it blooms the first time, keep it in bright shade and quite cool, under 70 in the daytime and under 50 at night. Mist the buds with luke-warm water. Remove each flower the minute it fades. When the plant is through flowering, keep it indoors until all danger of frost is past, then put it in the outdoor garden in its pot. Don't worry if it looks dead.

Bring it in just before the first frost and repot it. Make sure there is plenty of gravel for drainage in the bottom of the pot. The bulb should be covered by about 2 inches of soil. Water thoroughly, and continue to keep the soil slightly damp. The pot should be in direct sunshine, but night-time temperatures should fall below 60. Be patient. Eventually the scraggly leaved stem will emerge and grow tall. It will probably need staking. Soon a bud or buds will appear and open into the beautiful, sweet-smelling blossom we are all familiar with.

GERANIUM (*Pelargonium*)
Nobody calls geraniums *Pelargoniums,* although true geraniums are entirely different plants. Everybody grows them, which might make you think it's easy. It is.

Geraniums now come in a dazzling array of sizes and colors of blooms and even various scents of foliage. They are usually started from stem cuttings, but you can buy seeds for many varieties from the usual sources. Starting from seed, usually done in January, is superior in one way: Viral diseases can be transmitted and multiplied by repeated cuttings from the same plant.

Geraniums come in all sizes. Dwarfs are best for indoor cultivation. Geraniums want lots of light, water, and fertilizer during the season of greatest growth. If you put them outside in the summer, keep them in pots, on a porch or deck, and deadhead and prune off straggly growth occasionally. Although many growers do not, I give mine a period of rest after bringing them in in the fall, cutting them back and giving them little light and minimal water.

Fig. 63. Geranium.

GLOXINIA (*Sinningia*)

Gloxinias and African violets are cousins; I think gloxinias are prettier, with their larger, bell-like, warm red flowers. They like about the same culture as African violets with some important differences. African violets bloom more or less all year long; gloxinias need a period of dormancy after a period of bloom.

When blooms start to fade, treat the plant, in general, like any other plant going into a dormant period. Don't feed it, decrease watering gradually, and keep it in an area of lower light. Finally, the leaves will fall off. Don't do anything; wait. After two months or more, the plant will start to grow again. At this point, repot it, and resume feeding every month and bottom watering often enough to keep the soil barely moist.

Gloxinias, unlike African violets, should never have wet leaves. Not only that, when bottom watered, they should be removed from the water as soon as the top surface of the soil becomes moist. They can be propagated from leaf petiole cuttings or grown from seed.

IMPATIENS (*Impatiens*)

Called nowadays mostly by their Latin name, impatiens used to be called Patient Lucy or Busy Lizzie. (Don't expect gardeners to be consistent.) They are available in a wide variety of colors and types, and are easy to grow from cuttings in early fall or seed in January. I don't grow them indoors because they are so attractive to all kinds of insects, particularly aphids and mites.

They must have shade outdoors in summer, but in the winter greenhouse there is seldom too much light for them. They don't like the soil to dry out, and they thrive at normal house temperatures, which means nights about 60 and days about 70. Given these conditions, they will flower all year long and live a long time, if the bugs don't get them.

MORNING GLORY (*Ipomoea*)

Morning glories are among many common garden plants greenhousers would never think of growing indoors, but they will do well and add color and cheer to the late-fall greenhouse. Plant a half dozen seeds in a pot outdoors in the garden in late August. When the seedlings emerge, thin to the best three. Keep the pot out as late in the year as possible, on a porch or deck in direct sun, but be careful: Morning glories die at the first touch of frost. Bring the pot into the greenhouse when you have to, and place it in full sun. Provide a trellis for them to grow on, keep the soil moist, and give them a dilute liquid fertilizer once a month or so.

NASTURTIUM (*Tropaeolum*)

Nasturtiums do better in the cool, sunny greenhouse than in the house. Some gardeners turn up their noses at them, regarding them as coarse in appearance (and perhaps too easy to grow), but they are currently profiting from the fad for edible flowers. All parts of the plant can be used in salads, although the leaves are quite peppery.

Nasturtiums come in pretty much any shade except blue. Tall ones are climbers; I have seen a nasturtium vine 5 feet long with beautiful flowers, growing in nothing but a glass of water. Dwarf varieties make good hanging plants. Either kind will be all leaves and no flowers if given too much nitrogen.

Grow them from seed sown in September and they'll brighten your greenhouse in November. Some books

Fig. 64. Nasturtium.

recommend the nasturtium as a plant that repels insects. The authors obviously have not seen the way it attracts aphids. I use it in the garden as a trap plant.

POINSETTIA (*Euphorbia pulcherrima*)

Almost everyone gets a poinsettia, or several, at Christmas, and then throws it away. Your friends will give you lots of poinsettias in January. They are very easy to keep growing but somewhat hard to get to bloom again. To do this, in late September start giving them ten hours of bright light and fourteen hours of total darkness every day for six weeks, and keep them warm (65 degrees) at night. That's not hard, is it? Remember, if they receive any light at all at night, the whole procedure is shot.

Cheer up. One year I put a poinsettia out in the garden all summer, in the ground, not in a pot, which is wrong. I ripped it up (the roots spread like wildfire), potted it, and brought it into the greenhouse about September 15, before the first frost. It bloomed, but not right at Christmas and not as brilliantly as a florist's. I think the reason it bloomed at all is that October and November were very cloudy that year.

The rest of the year, poinsettias need bright light and cool temperatures. They should dry out between waterings. They get leggy; prune them in May. Put them out in summer. If you don't care about making the bracts turn red, they're no trouble at all.

ROSE (*Rosa*)

You can't grow regular roses indoors, at least not easily, but you can grow miniatures. These grow anywhere from 6 to 14 inches high and are available in all the colors found on regular roses. They are well suited to greenhouse culture, liking the cool nights and warmish days of the greenhouse and as much full sun as possible. They will do all right with less sun but will not bloom as much.

They have one advantage over outdoor roses: They bloom all year long, typically having a spurt of bloom, then a dormant period, then another spurt. Cut them back severely after each spurt. Buy them at a florist or from catalogs. If they come bare-rooted, pot them up, prune off the tips, and leave them in the shade for a few days. Feed them with dilute liquid fertilizer fairly frequently; keep the soil moist but not wet. Propagate from tip cuttings.

OTHER FLOWERS

Many garden flowers, such as petunias, browallia, nicotiana, ageratum, and others, will continue to flower for a few months if you bring them into the greenhouse (after a quarantine period) before the first frost. Look for self-sown seedlings around the base of the mother plant.

Nonflowering Houseplants

Although every plant flowers, except some primitive types like ferns, "nonflowering" houseplants for the purposes of this book are those that either don't flower under the usual conditions of temperature, humidity, and light in a house or greenhouse or have flowers that are so tiny or odd that they are usually overlooked.

It is always difficult to categorize living things. Geraniums and begonias are certainly flowering houseplants, but some varieties are treasured more for their foliage than for their blooms; some geraniums are even considered herbs because of the scent of their leaves.

ORIGINS OF FOLIAGE PLANTS

Many of the plants listed below originated in a jungle or swamp environment. If you think about the conditions under which your houseplants originated, you can probably figure out how to grow them. Most of them do not like a great deal of bright sunshine, but prefer indirect (natural) light such as that provided on a north windowsill or by sunlight filtered through a lace curtain. However, it is good to remember that during the darkest months, even an uncurtained south window may not get all that much sunlight. If these plants are put outside in summer, as many can be, they should be placed in light shade.

Many of these foliage plants do best in soil that never dries out totally but is always moist. At the same time, they do not like to have "wet feet," that is, to stand in saturated soil. Many prefer more humidity than is available in the average home in winter, which means they require frequent misting and may be best in pots that rest on moist pebbles. Rather than go into great and repetitious detail, these conditions are summarized below by the term "moist shade," and the temperatures preferred by many foliage plants are called "house temperatures," which means temperatures that seldom go below 65 degrees at night and can be 80 or so in the daytime. Plants in this category don't do well in the usual greenhouse that dips below 60 at night, but they will thrive in a greenhouse that is warmer than that. Other foliage plants like "normal" greenhouse temperatures.

BOSTON FERN (*Nephrolepis*)
You could call the Boston fern the most eminent of the Victorians; no proper nineteenth-century city home was without one. They were kept on beautiful wooden fern stands that are now collector's items. The stands allowed the fronds to cascade down; a hanging pot will perform the same service.

Unlike maidenhair or staghorn, this fern looks the way most people think a fern ought to look. It likes soil with plenty of humus to which a bit of bone meal could be added, and good drainage. It wants bright shade and high humidity but can stand nighttime temperatures down to 55, which means it can be grown in a cool greenhouse. Don't touch it; the touched frond will turn brown.

Give these plants a feeding of dilute liquid fertilizer only every six months or so. Even then, beware; they grow fast. When the plant gets too big or turns brown in the center, lift it, divide it, cut out the brown part, and give half to a friend.

BURRO'S TAIL (*Sedum*)
Burro's or donkey's tail is a succulent, and like most succulents, it is very hard to kill. Give it full sun or bright shade and any temperature above freezing, and it will last for years if not overwatered. It grows vigorously through the summer and has a period of dormancy in the winter, during which it should be watered only if the fat blue-green leaves are observed to shrivel.

Feed it very sparingly, and not at all from October to April. To propagate, break off a group of two or three leaves and insert the torn end a very short distance into damp sand. Rooting will take place in less than a week.

COLEUS (*Coleus*)

One of the most beautiful foliage plants, with leaves of many colors, but mostly green to russet, coleus has been grown as a houseplant for many years. It is easy to grow in full sun or shade but will have better color in the shade. It likes house temperatures, 65 at night and as hot as you like in the daytime. Soil should be always moist. In a cool greenhouse, coleus will live but may become dormant until nights get warmer.

Fig. 65. Coleus.

Coleus are fast growers and may be started from tiny seeds, but it's better to buy your first one. Later, if you like, you can root cuttings in a glass of water. Coleus come in a wide range of foliage colors and types. If you don't like the look of the pale blue flowers a coleus occasionally produces, just pinch them off as they appear.

DRACAENA (*Dracaena*)

Usually called by its Latin name, dracaena (pronounced "drah-SEE-na"), comes in many types and sizes. All like house temperatures and bright, moist conditions. This and many similar plants can come to look like a cartoon palm tree as the lower leaves drop, leaving a crown of stiff leaves like those given out in some churches on Palm Sunday. The thing to do then is to air-layer the stem and start over. If you have a *Dracaena draco,* a dragon tree, you have a specimen of the oldest living thing on earth. Forget the redwoods; one dragon tree in its natural Canary Island setting was estimated to be six thousand years old.

ENGLISH IVY (*Hedera*)

There are thousands of true ivies, as well as other plants called "ivy" but botanically quite different. All are easy to grow. If you are familiar with the English climate, try to

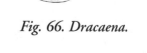

Fig. 66. Dracaena.

duplicate it or come close indoors by giving ivy bright, indirect light and nights in the 50s and days in the 60s. Ivies will tolerate almost any light conditions and quite cold temperatures but hate extreme heat. They should be fed sparingly and misted; in fact, if mites are a problem, give them frequent showers (if the plants are small enough to be portable), using warm soapy water, then rinsing.

Ivies can be kept in hanging pots or trained up a stake or wall, as long as it is not too smooth. If you pinch them back to keep them full, the stems pinched off can be rooted easily.

JADE PLANT (*Crassula argentea*)

I don't remember who gave us a jade plant, or when. It now stands about 3 feet high and weighs, with pot, something over 100 pounds. It would be bigger, but I stopped feeding it and refused to repot it when repotting became a job that would tax an 800-pound gorilla. We keep it on a dolly so we can wheel it out of the greenhouse onto the deck in summer. Cluttering up the greenhouse are about twenty of its babies; we could have had five hundred if we desired.

Jade plants are succulents, which means that they can go a long time without water because their thick, fleshy leaves retain it. They are easy to care for—water them or don't; feed them or don't; give them direct sun or shade; wheel them outside or keep them in. They can survive in temperature extremes of 100 degrees or just above freezing.

Don't think we don't love our jade plant. Because we leave it in direct sun all summer, its leaves have red-tinged edges. Since it is an old plant and receives full sun, it blooms, producing exquisite tiny, white, star-shaped flowers. Jade plants are said to be susceptible to mealybugs; ours doesn't seem to be susceptible to anything.

Fig. 67. Jade plant.

KALANCHOE (*Kalanchoe*)

There are many kalanchoes ("kal-uhn-koes" or "kal-uhn-ko-ees"), and they vary a great deal in appearance. K. mortagei is known as mother-of-hundreds, since about that many babies grow along the edges of the leaves

Fig. 68. Kalanchoe.

and then drop off. K. tomentosa is called the panda plant, probably because of its woolly leaves. It occasionally sends up a few less-than-gorgeous flowers but is usually kept as a foliage plant.

K. blossfeldiana is pretty or bizarre looking, depending on your tastes. It produces quite small, red, four-petaled, trumpet-shaped blooms on odd stalks that shoot off from the stems. This, of course, makes it a flowering houseplant, but other kalanchoes are basically foliage plants, so all are listed here. Specimens are sold quite inexpensively by florists for Christmas blooming. Most of them are crosses between *K. blossfeldiana* and another kalanchoe and are superior to both parents.

All kalanchoes are succulent or semisucculent. *K. blossfeldiana* leaves are like those of the jade plant, except that some of them are bluntly serrated while others are not. Stems are like jade stems, brown and woody, but even more twisted and gnarled. Like any succulent, it needs limited waterings and should dry out in between. It likes a well-drained soil mix, perhaps half sand, and does best in less than full sun.

One authority says you should buy kalanchoes, let them bloom, and then throw them away, because they are almost impossible to bring into bloom again. I stuck mine outdoors all summer, brought it in in the fall, pruned it a bit, and it bloomed again. Since most are hybrids, growing them from seed is not practical, but they are easy to grow from cuttings. Normally, they will bloom in midwinter; to get them to bloom for Christmas, treat them like poinsettias.

MAIDENHAIR FERN (*Adiantum*)

Oddly, *Adiantum* looks nothing like a maiden's hair, at least not any maiden I ever knew, nor does it look "ferny" like a Boston fern. Instead, the leaves are rounded lobes. There are several varieties. All need more humidity than is readily available in most homes, so they will thrive in a cool, humid greenhouse, especially one that is not too hot in the daytime.

Maidenhairs are real swamp plants and need a growing medium that contains lots of humus to hold moisture and is constantly wet. In winter, they may be allowed to dry out a bit. Like many ferns, they don't like to be touched and are propagated by division.

MOTHER-IN-LAW'S TONGUE (*Dieffenbachia*)
Like many other plants, this is now often called by its Latin name, even by laymen. Terms like wandering Jew and mother-in-law's tongue just don't seem "nice" in our wimpy age. Another common name for *Dieffenbachia* is dumbcane, referring to the fact that those who chew the leaves of this plant will find it very hard to speak; they will also be quite ill. Don't let the family cat eat *Dieffenbachia,* and it's probably better not to have it in a house with small children.

This plant is in the common "house temperatures, bright shade" category, but unlike most in this category, it should be allowed to dry out completely between waterings. There are many attractive varieties; most feature dark green leaves with white markings. Like *Dracaena,* it can grow straggly and be restarted through air layering or cane cuttings.

NORFOLK ISLAND PINE (*Araucaria*)
Norfolk Island pine is another of those popular, grow-anywhere, can't-kill-'em plants. I have seen more than one in a bathroom, where it appears to enjoy the humidity and low light, although the ones I've seen were in bathrooms that at least had a window. They will grow equally well in full sun and like nights in the 50s and days in the 60s but will stand lower or higher temperatures.

They are sometimes bought as Christmas trees, then kept for years. They will grow a few inches a year if soil is always barely moist and feedings occur every three months. They are easy to propagate from tip cuttings, but taking such a cutting will cause the top to divide into several branches, making the tree less shapely. Some owners do this when the plant is quite old and has lost its lower branches, then throw away the original plant.

PEPEROMIA (*Peperomia*)
Peperomia has nothing to do with pepper. Most such names, like poinsettia and *Dieffenbachia,* honor a long-dead botanist. There are a number of

varieties of peperomia. All are typical jungle plants, which means that they thrive in house temperatures and light conditions, but they are succulents, which means that the only way to kill them is to overwater them. The leaves are more "leafy," that is, less thick and swollen, than those of the jade plant or kalanchoe. Some are wrinkled, some smooth; most are dark green with stripes of silver or white.

Blossoms may protrude above the canopy of foliage, but they won't look much like flowers but more like caterpillars or Fourth-of-July "punk." Wrinkled-leaf types can be propagated from leaf cuttings, others from stem cuttings. This plant is not as common as some of the others, and some commercial growers may not have it.

PHILODENDRON (*Philodendron*)

Which is the most popular of all houseplants is debatable, but in any contest, the philodendron would be right up there. Perhaps its most endearing characteristic is this: If you give it perfect conditions for growth, it will fill a small room in a few years, but if that idea doesn't appeal, keep it cooler and don't feed it, and it will remain a relatively small potted plant forever.

There are hundreds and hundreds of species of philodendrons, and plant breeders are creating more every day, but the saddle-leaved, which looks something like a Swiss cheese plant (*Monstera deliciosa*) and the heart-leaf, which has leaves shaped roughly as the name suggests, are among the most popular. Heart-leafs are vines; the leaves will stay fairly small if the plant is not given any support to climb on but become huge if it is. The saddle-leaved and similar philodendrons grow from a crown that is in soil, but they can become just about as large, wider if not so high.

All species like the usual bright, indirect light, soil always moist but not wet, nights above 60 degrees, and feeding three or four times a year. Those are what you give them if you want giants. With poorer conditions, they will do a bit less well, but they're hard to kill and will grow in plain water for years, or in just peat moss. The vines can be propagated from stem cuttings; the saddle-leaved and similar species can be grown from seed. From time to time, dust should be wiped from the leaves of either kind with a damp cloth wrung out in tepid water. This is a good practice with almost any glossy-leaved houseplant.

PINEAPPLE (*Ananas*)

Most people have seen a plant growing from a sweet potato or avocado seed on a windowsill; not so many know that you can grow pineapples at home. You'll get more pleasure than fruit out of the activity, however. Pineapples are bromeliads. These are New World plants, many of which are spiny epiphytes (air plants), which means they grow on other plants but are not parasites. Pineapples are spiny but not epiphytic.

Buy an underripe pineapple and cut off the top $^1/_2$ inch, with the leaves on. Hollow out the part you cut off so that there is nothing but skin and leaves left. Dust it with rooting compound if you wish. Dry it in the sun for two weeks. Set it about 2 inches deep in a soil made of half peat moss, a quarter commercial potting soil, and a quarter sand. Leave it in direct sun. Keep the soil moist but not wet; it helps to mist it with tepid water fairly regularly, but not every day. It will grow.

If you want to get it to blossom, put the whole thing into a big, clear plastic bag and add one or two ripe apples. Like many fruits, apples give off a gas as they ripen that affects the growth of other plants. In a few months, your pineapple will flower; some time later, believe it or not, you'll be able to pick small, edible pineapples.

SENSITIVE PLANT (*Mimosa pudica*)

Children love all kinds of gardening, and no activity could be better for them. You might want to keep a few plants that intrigue them—not to mention us. Sensitive plant is a quite small, fernlike plant that occasionally puts forth a small puffy pink or purple bloom but is kept for the curious behavior of its leaves. If a branch is touched, the leaves will curl up; if touched hard enough, the plant will droop, although it has not suffered any real damage.

Sensitive plant likes moist, bright shade but can be a bit drier in winter. *M. pudica* can be started from seed; commercial growers sometimes give one away as a "loss leader." It can be put outside in summer and thrives at any temperature that doesn't go below 50 at night.

Fig. 69. Sensitive plant.

SWISS CHEESE PLANT (*Monstera deliciosa*)

This is often called nowadays by its Latin name and is equally often mis-called split-leaf or cut-leaf philodendron. It resembles a philodendron but is not one. It's easy to grow. How easy is it? Our eight-year-old daughter sent away for one advertised in the back of a comic book or some such publication. It came shoved partway into a plastic test tube, and I knew it would die. Ten years later, I gave it to a museum. It took three men and a pickup truck to get it there.

Fig. 70. Swiss cheese plant.

It scared me. It was in our den, a dimly lit room with one east and one south window, both shaded. It grew in a huge pot, up a bamboo pole, over the ceiling and some walls, while air roots hung down and crept across the carpet. I could feel it looking at me late at night, and I thought some morning my family would find my chair empty.

That explains the "monstera" part. One book says the "deliciosa" fruit is poisonous; others say it's good eating. Ours never produced fruit, but if it had, I wouldn't have touched it. Botanists say it needs house temperatures and bright, moist conditions and should be fed twice a year. If the room or greenhouse it's in goes below 60 degrees, it may not grow as well, which might not be all bad. If it gets straggly and you actually want more of them, cut it back to the base, from which it will grow again, and make cuttings from sections of stem that have at least one leaf. The museum thought it was great.

SPIDER PLANT (*Chlorophytum*)

There are spiderwort, spider lilies, and spider flowers (*Cleome*), but *Chlorophytum* is usually called spider plant or spider ivy, although it may also be called ribbon plant. It is one of the most commonly grown foliage plants, almost always grown in a hanging pot, since it is the stereotypical "baby"-producing plant. It sends out runners that, with or without soil, produce a miniature spider plant every few inches. All you need to do to propagate it is to pin the baby spider into a pot, and cut the runner when it takes root. Florists don't sell many of these. Everybody gets one from a friend.

They are, obviously, easy to grow, but it's hard to grow a top-notch specimen. Soil should be moist all the time, a requirement many house-holders find difficult, since it usually involves standing on a chair. Not only that, they are very sensitive to fluorides or other chemicals in tap water. They like cool nights and bright shade, so they can be kept on the north side of the greenhouse. Use commercial houseplant potting soil and commercial houseplant liquid fertilizer, or fish emulsion or manure tea, very dilute, not oftener than every three months. If the brown tips bother you, prune them off.

STAGHORN FERN (*Platycerium bifurcatum*)
Staghorn fern takes a bit of trouble to get started, but it is spectacular if not beautiful when it attains full growth. You see these in barrooms and hunting lodges; they look like a pair of green antlers.

To start one, you need a slab of bark. Gouge out a hole in it, fill the hole with compost and some peat moss, and keep it moist. Put the plant, which you probably purchased, in the medium. You may need to tie it on at first, but in a few weeks the lower leaves will have turned brown and curled around the bark, helping to hold the plant in place.

Staghorns should be watered about every other week and frequently misted. About the only way you can fertilize them is to put liquid fertil-izer, very dilute, in the mister. Feed sparingly. The staghorn thrives in almost no light and may produce babies on one side or the other, which you can give away to someone else who wants a staghorn fern.

VENUS FLYTRAP (*Dionaea muscipula*)
If kids like the sensitive plant, they'll love the Venus flytrap, but it may gross out their parents. It originated in swampy soil that didn't provide nourishment, so it and similar plants became carnivorous. The unwary fly that lands on the two-lobed leaf will cause it to snap shut like a clam, trapping him, after which the plant secretes what amount to digestive juices.

Venus flytrap requires about the same conditions as the sensitive plant, but it likes high temperatures less. Don't give it fertilizer; it can't use it. You may be able to feed it bits of hamburger, but live flies are best. Unfortunately, it never seems to eat an aphid. If you have kids that don't mind crippling flies and dropping them on the leaves, it will thrive. It doesn't do well with dead ones.

WANDERING JEW (*Tradescantia* or *Zebrina*)

Wandering Jew can be either of two plants, botanically, but they are so similar that it makes little difference to us. Its name is said to have no religious significance. It was a popular plant in the last century, before you could buy plants in every supermarket. Most people got them from friends, and wandering Jew traveled in a few months from Boston to New York to Philadelphia, like the itinerant Central European peddlers of old.

Like most old-fashioned plants, wandering Jew likes bright shade, but it is somewhat different in that it prefers cool nights and likes dry soil between waterings. It is usually kept in hanging pots so that the foliage can trail downward. The markings on the basically green leaves can vary from leaf to leaf on the same plant. To propagate, take a stem cutting and shove it in some moist soil in a pot. That's all.

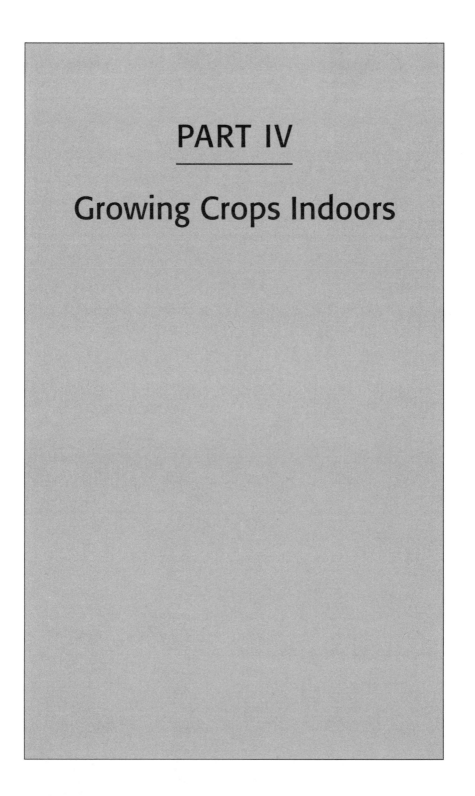

PART IV

Growing Crops Indoors

Growing Greenhouse Crops

If asked, most greenhousers will probably say that they never grow crops indoors; that is, they use the greenhouse only for starting seedlings to be transplanted into the outdoor garden, possibly with a small amount of additional use for housing or propagating houseplants. If you press them, however, they will remember the pot of basil or parsley that they take snippets from in winter, or the lettuce thinnings they ate last spring.

Any discussion of growing crops indoors to a greater degree than that, for example, to the degree that you try to feed your family with what you raise in the greenhouse in the wintertime, can, believe it or not, become quite controversial. In fact, it can verge on religious argument. On the one hand, there are those whose greenhouses lie empty from July to March because they use them only for starting seeds in the spring. On the other hand, there are those who depend on their own crops grown year-round in the greenhouse, such as the disciples of Helen and Scott Nearing.

Most readers probably fall somewhere between these two poles—that is, they would like to grow a few flowers, vegetables, and herbs in the colder months, but they don't plan to subsist exclusively on what can be produced in the greenhouse in winter.

You may have been a gardener a long time, and you may have had a good deal of experience in starting seeds in your greenhouse for transplanting into the garden, but those experiences will not have prepared you for growing crops indoors. It's fun to try, but expect frustration. Most northern greenhouses just don't have enough light and heat in winter without artificial aids, and artificial aids can let you down. You will learn by experience what you can and can't do in your particular situation.

INDOOR AND OUTDOOR CLIMATES

If you want to produce crops, to whatever degree, in the greenhouse, you will need a much better understanding of the climate of your particular greenhouse than is necessary just to start seeds in the spring. This climate depends on two factors: the outdoor climate where you live and the nature and construction of your greenhouse.

Freestanding Greenhouse Climate

If you have a typical freestanding greenhouse, chances are that most of the year it is too hot in the daytime and too cold at night to grow most plants. Unless it has numerous expensive mechanical heating and ventilation devices, its chief use is to extend the growing season. Especially with a little bit of artificial help when needed, you can start seeds in it in late February or March and keep plants growing in it until October or early November.

If you live in an area with a mild climate, for example, a nonmountainous part of Virginia, you can extend the above schedule for something like another thirty days on each end, which means that you can grow things in your freestanding greenhouse throughout the coolest months. You could, that is, if temperature were the only thing that mattered and light were not a consideration.

No matter where you live, your freestanding greenhouse will almost certainly be too hot inside during the summer to grow most crops. This isn't much of a drawback, since you can grow plants outdoors at that time.

Attached Greenhouse Climate

If you have an attached greenhouse with little or no glass in the roof, it will behave in almost the opposite fashion. It will not be too hot inside in the summer, because the high angle of the sun in the sky will keep sunlight inside the greenhouse to a minimum. The difficulty with growing crops inside in summer, or in early fall when you are more likely to wish to do so, will be a lack of light.

Climatic Variation

The U.S. climate varies tremendously from one locality to another. Far more than we realize, we are creatures of our environment. Where I live, in upstate New York, 6 miles from the Vermont line, winters are cold and dark, but not uniformly so. November is a terribly dreary month. We are scheduled to receive nine to ten hours of sunlight, but we get only about 40 percent of that. December days are even shorter, although not much, but we receive more like 50 percent of available sunlight.

February, on the other hand, has days that are ten to eleven hours long, and we receive 60 percent or more of the sunlight we should get. From the middle of February on, we can actually sit out on a south-facing roof on a sunny day and get a tan, and not just on hands and face. Climate can be very local; there are areas less than 50 miles from us that receive 20 percent less sunlight in February.

Our daughter lives in Santa Fe. Although her location is more than a mile higher than ours, the average daily temperature there in winter is about 10 degrees warmer. More to the point for greenhousers, the sun shines about one hour longer per day from November to February and, most important of all, Santa Fe receives 70 percent or more of that light in all the winter months.

You may say, "Well, of course, everybody knows that," but there is a difference between knowing things intellectually and absorbing them internally. One of the better books on greenhouse growing, written about twenty years ago, was compiled by people whose greenhouse experience was largely acquired in the desert Southwest. In reading it, I find myself constantly saying, "What are they talking about? You can't do that!" What I meant was, "I can't do that!"

If you live in a sunnier winter climate than mine, as you read what follows, you may say the opposite: "I can do much better than that!" There are, however, climates even worse than ours for greenhousing, like the Pacific Northwest or the Northern Great Lakes area. In the last analysis, you will have to learn from experience, aided by climate information compiled by the U.S. government, just what you can and can't do in your greenhouse.

INSOLATION

Insolation, not to be confused with insulation, is a term used by meteorologists and solar engineers. It means the amount of sunlight that falls on a given location during a given period. To find out the length of any given day in your area, consult an almanac. To find out the average percentage of possible sunlight your area receives during each month of the year, call the weather bureau at the nearest good-size airport or major city near you. If they can't help you, write to the National Renewable Energy Laboratories, 1617 Cole Blvd., Golden, CO 80401-3393. Ask them to consult the *Maximum-Minimum Daily and Direct Normal Solar Radiation Manual*. If you want to get into this seriously, tell them you want to buy a copy of the manual.

If you're into websites, punch up www.ncdc.noaa.gov, or call (704) 271-4800, extension 2. Either of those actions will get you the U.S. Government Climatological Office in Asheville, North Carolina.

SOLAR SEASONS

To better understand how and, more important, when to grow food, flowers, and herbs in your greenhouse, it may help to think of the year as divided, not into conventional seasons, but into solar seasons. If you are a gardener, and especially if you are a greenhouser, you have undoubtedly noticed that the heating of the earth by the sun has a time lag. Your garden receives exactly the same number of hours of sunlight on March 21 as it does on September 21, but it's much, much colder in March. In a well-constructed attached greenhouse, however, the temperature produced by the sunlight will be more or less the same on both days, which is what you need to remember in planning for indoor crops.

Thinking in terms of solar seasons, as many meteorologists and solar engineers do, helps you understand *what* you can grow *when* in an attached greenhouse with little or no roof glazing. Solar spring is from early February to early May. Plants will grow very rapidly during the first part of this period, as the hours of sunlight increase, and continue to thrive until the end of it.

Solar summer is from early May to early August. While it continues to grow warmer outside, the amount of sunlight entering through south windows is at a minimum. Plants remaining indoors will have to be placed close to these windows, or even moved each day, to take advantage of sunlight entering east and west windows.

Solar fall is from early August to early November. You can get a great deal of growth out of plants during this period, but in August and early September, the greenhouse will be hot unless thoroughly ventilated, since

Fig. 71. Because the summer sun strikes the earth at a high angle, sunlight does not enter greenhouse windows as directly as in fall, and the greenhouse doesn't overheat.

now a lower solar angle coincides with higher outdoor temperatures. Often the solution to this problem is to move plants into, or start them in, the outdoor garden, moving them inside in late September or early October.

Solar winter is from early November to early February. This is the toughest time in the greenhouse, if your climate is roughly the same as or worse than upstate New York. You may need artificial light or heat, probably both, to bring crops to fruition in November and December or to start early-spring crops in December and January.

For most of us greenhousers who live in Canada or the northern United States (roughly, north of the latitude of Washington, D.C.), crop growing is done in late fall and early spring. There is no need to grow crops indoors in summer, unless you are the rare person with a greenhouse and no garden, and growing most things in the dead of winter takes more time and energy, human and electrical, than we care to spend.

This doesn't mean that the greenhouse lies useless in December. In addition to the houseplants living there, mostly in a state of slow growth or near dormancy, there may be crops just reaching the end of their growth period, with or without artificial light and heat, and seeds being started, almost certainly with artificial light and probably with artificial heat, for very early-spring crops.

COOL-WEATHER CROPS

A surprising number of plants commonly grown in the garden will withstand quite low temperatures if they receive enough light; some can do quite well even under cloudy and cool conditions. Most of these are brassicas, such as Chinese or regular cabbage, but they include other plants grown for their leaves, like lettuce or spinach, and scallions. Many root crops, such as parsnips or beets, will also thrive in cool conditions, but the average gardener may feel that it is more practical to store these in winter than to grow them.

Almost all plants commonly grown to produce cut flowers will do well in a cool greenhouse, if it doesn't go below 40 degrees too far or too frequently. Many will do better under these conditions than in the garden in July or August. To produce masses of blooms, however, most flowers require a considerable amount of light.

WARM-WEATHER CROPS

Other crops, first and foremost tomatoes, and their cousins peppers and eggplant, like more heat than is usually available in the northern winter greenhouse. Unfortunately, tomatoes also fall into the category of vegetables that don't store well and aren't available in supermarkets in winter. (Well, yes, they are available, but we all know what they taste like, and unfortunately, we often don't know what they've been sprayed with.) Most of us will probably try, therefore, to grow some heat-loving plants in the winter greenhouse.

Although they will probably not bear as heavily as in the summer garden, you may be able to have at least a few homegrown tomatoes throughout most of the year by following the suggestions in the next chapter. The same is true of peppers and eggplant. For winter growth in the greenhouse, look for varieties of plants designed for growth in the South. Though it may be hot there, summer days are shorter than in the North, and plant breeders have developed varieties adapted to short-day culture. Sometimes these varieties will do well in the northern winter greenhouse.

TIME TO MATURITY

In planning for indoor crops, bear in mind that the estimated time to maturity, such as 65 days, usually listed in seed catalogs and sometimes on packets, refers to the time that the plant will require to reach maturity under optimum conditions. If conditions are cooler than that, and especially if they are darker, it may take much longer, up to twice as long in some cases.

For this reason, ideal greenhouse vegetable crops are often those that can be eaten before maturity, which generally means those that are grown for their leaves, like lettuce and Chinese (but not regular) cabbage, or certain ones grown for their roots, like turnips and radishes. When you thin lettuce plants that are 2 inches high, you can and should eat the thinnings. Unfortunately, there are no flowers that can be picked before maturity, at least not more than a few days before.

SPECIAL GREENHOUSE VARIETIES

There is one problem you probably aren't prepared for that will astonish you. Most garden varieties will do all right started in winter and finished in spring; provided with artificial heat and light, they will come to fruition during the long days of spring. But many varieties of flowers and vegetables that grow beautifully for you in the garden just won't produce in the greenhouse. Mostly, these are plants grown for their fruit or swollen roots or for their flowers. Plants that need a certain length of day to trigger bloom, fruiting, or the swelling of roots or stems may or may not produce if started in late summer or early fall, because they will come to fruition during very short days. There are varieties of these specifically bred for greenhouse culture, however, and I have listed all those I could find in the chapters that follow. Often their seeds are harder to obtain and much more expensive than ordinary seeds. It's fun and practical to try to grow crops in the greenhouse, but expect a higher failure rate.

Seed companies are there to help you. Don't hesitate to call one or more to ask which of their varieties they recommend for indoor growing, especially in short-day or low-light conditions. You will be helped by the fact that you will want this information in fall, which is not their busy season. Never call a seed company for advice between January 1 and June 1; that's like calling a florist for advice the day before Mother's Day. Your local florists or commercial greenhousers also may help if you approach them right. You may be able to beg, borrow, or buy some special seed from a commercial grower, or at least get some excellent and free advice.

The chapters that follow discuss specific vegetables, herbs, and flowers that can be grown to maturity in the fall, spring, and in some cases, winter greenhouse, and the varieties best suited for this culture.

Vegetable Crops

You can grow anything indoors, in almost any climate, if you're willing to expend the necessary time, money, and energy. I assume that most readers of this book will not choose to grow vegetables that require a tremendous amount of space or that can easily be grown in summer and stored, either as frozen food or in some other manner. Nothing is impossible, but growing corn in a home greenhouse is extremely unlikely.

VEGETABLES THAT CAN BE STORED OR FROZEN
Potatoes, carrots, beets, and other roots can be stored fairly easily in a root cellar or other cool, reasonably dry place. Besides that, you can take parsnips and carrots out of the garden all winter. Brush the snow off the row that you remembered to mark carefully, remove a few feet of mulch, then dig (or dynamite), and if the mice haven't gotten them, they'll be all right.

Winter squash got its name because it stores easily. Most homegrown vegetables, particularly summer squash, broccoli, peas, beans, corn, spinach, and Brussels sprouts, can be home frozen in such a way that they taste nearly like fresh produce. So what's left, in the way of vegetables, that's worth the time and trouble to grow in the home greenhouse? Quite a bit.

COOL-WEATHER CROPS
All of the vegetables described below can be grown in the fall greenhouse with little or no artificial heat or light. Or, started in winter with a small

amount of artificial help, they will mature about the time you would be putting in peas outdoors (if you start peas when I do, while there is still some snow on the ground).

Lettuce

An excellent vegetable to grow in the greenhouse is lettuce, in all its myriad varieties, along with its cousins. By November, it may be hard to find decent lettuce in the supermarket, and what you can buy has been sprayed with God knows what, but lettuce in your greenhouse will be excellent. By Christmas, unless you're really fortunate or skillful, it will all be gone.

Most leaf lettuce matures in forty-five to sixty days, but it can take much longer when daylight hours are shorter. It has one advantage, however, shared by all leafy vegetables: You can eat it at any stage. If you have to thin it, eat the thinnings. If you pick one or two leaves to eat from each mature plant, it will last practically forever.

Fig. 72. Leaf lettuce.

Head lettuce or semihead lettuce, like butterhead, takes longer than leaf lettuce and is harder to grow. The rule is, the more solid the head, the longer it takes, and the more difficult it is. There is satisfaction in growing a head of iceberg, but in my opinion it can't compare in flavor with Red Sails or Simpson's.

One of the main problems you may experience in growing lettuce is too much heat; it will bolt quickly if the temperature is too high. For fall crops, it may be better to start seeds in an outdoor seed bed. Start in mid-August and make *small* plantings, not more than twenty seeds of all kinds, every two weeks. Seedlings can be transplanted into small pots in the garden soil. Take them into the greenhouse about the time of first frost. Lettuce is one of those plants that not only transplant easily, but seem actually to do better if transplanted.

Indoors, start seeds in a shallow bed or flat, but be sure soil temperatures don't rise above 65. Lettuce seed will germinate at 45 degrees or less, but at such low temperatures it will take longer. It is supposed to need light to germinate, but I find it does fine if covered lightly. Wherever lettuce was started, it can be grown in the greenhouse in large pots or a bed about 8 inches deep. It likes plenty of water, but splashing the leaves may encourage disease. Pots are better in that they can be bottom watered, but they take up more space than beds. Incidentally, lettuce and other cool-weather crops don't particularly need to have their water warmed, at least not after they have left the seedling stage.

Lettuce can also be grown in early spring, using artificial light and heat at first if needed; the heat is less likely to be necessary. I find that early-spring lettuce doesn't do as well, probably because the greenhouse heats up in March and April with increased amounts of sunshine, but it's worth a try.

In addition to the varieties listed in chapter 7, you might want to consider the following: Titania is a head lettuce designed for greenhouse growth in spring, particularly for hydroponic growing. I have never tried it. Yvonne is a looseleaf lettuce bred especially for greenhouse growth. Ibis is a very dark red lettuce, many times darker than Red Sails, that grows very well in low-light conditions

Other Salad Greens

Mesclun, variously spelled and pronounced, is one of the hot gourmet items in fancy restaurants right now. By the time you read this, it may be passé. Used correctly, the term refers not to a specific green or greens but a method of growing. Buy mesclun mix from a seed house or mix it yourself, and scatter it sparingly over a bed that is 4 to 6 inches deep. When the various plants are about as high as the bed is deep, cut them with a scissors and use in salad. Most will continue to grow, providing you with further cuttings.

If you grow arugula, mache (corn salad), salad burnet, radicchio, sorrel, or any similar salad green outdoors, you can grow it in the greenhouse.

Spinach

Spinach will do well indoors but needs a great deal of space. Four square feet of well-grown spinach will cook down into about enough to provide one person with one meal. If you don't have that much space, eat it raw in salad. It tastes delicious and goes much farther that way.

Spinach is a close relative of the beet. Plant the beetlike seed about $1/2$ inch deep. In the greenhouse, don't plant it in rows but broadcast it. Space about 1 inch apart in every direction. It should not be necessary to thin spinach planted that way.

Spinach planted October 1 should be ready about mid-November. Or you might try starting spinach in late December or early January, giving it artificial light at first. Look for heat-resistant, not cold-resistant, varieties; spinach will withstand very low temperatures, but it's going to be warm in the greenhouse.

Traditional spinach has savoyed, or crinkly, leaves. Many people prefer this, but plain-leaved spinach is easier to wash, and sand is always a problem in spinach. Vienna is a heavily savoyed type, Tyee semisavoyed, and Bolero plain-leaved. All are good for greenhouse growing. Vienna matures in forty days, about ten days earlier than the other two; all are hybrids resistant to disease.

Swiss Chard

Swiss chard is perhaps the best of all vegetables to grow in the winter greenhouse, unless you happen to be among those, all too numerous, who don't care for it. Give it a try; homegrown chard tastes vastly different from store-bought. Like spinach, it is a close relative of the beet. Grow it about like spinach, but allow mature plants a little more room. It can be eaten cooked or raw and, like all greens, can be harvested before maturing. In other words, thin it and eat the thinnings.

There are white-veined, red-veined, and green-veined chard, but they all grow about the same way and taste about the same. The red, usually called rhubarb chard, takes a few days longer to maturity, and tastes nothing like rhubarb. Fordhook is the old standard variety of white.

Asian Greens

China, Japan, and Korea include areas that have very cold climates, and many splendid cool-weather vegetables originated there. "Chinese cabbage" now usually refers to michihili and similar plants, actually mustards that taste something like a cross between celery and cabbage. Michihili takes about eighty days to produce tall, large, self-blanched heads.

Pak choi or bok choy is less tall and harder to describe to someone who has never

Fig. 73. Chinese cabbage.

seen it. The leaves are spoon shaped, green above and white below. It takes only fifty days to maturity, but both pak choi and michihili can be eaten before maturity, in a salad or a stir-fry. Both are delicious, to my taste pak choi a little more so. The culture of both is similar to lettuce, but seeds should be planted deeper, covered with about a $1/4$ inch of soil. Young plants can be transplanted into 6- or 8-inch pots. Chinese cabbage is a bit more cold-hardy even than lettuce, but it can't stand heat.

Radishes

Radishes are everybody's favorite crop. They grow in all kinds of soil and conditions, and almost nothing matures faster. Sow radishes $1/4$ inch deep in a 4-inch-deep bed. Don't transplant. Thin to 1 to 2 inches apart if necessary. It usually takes about three weeks from planting the seed to eating the radish.

Radishes have only two drawbacks I know of. One is that some people don't like them, or think they don't, because they've never had good, sweet, fresh ones. The other is that varieties vary in their light requirements. If you sow long-day types in the fall greenhouse, they won't produce edible swollen roots. Plant Cherry Belle, a new kind called Cherriette, or Cavalier. You may have to shop around for Cavalier; many seed houses no longer sell it, because it will not produce under the long-day conditions of the spring garden, and some farmers and gardeners simply won't read directions.

Daikon is a Japanese white radish that can grow more than 8 inches long and is often cooked; Lo Bok is a similar Chinese radish. Daikon is hotter by far than Lo Bok and may not do as well in the greenhouse under low-light conditions.

Turnips

Turnips can be treated in every way like radishes but are seldom eaten raw, although they can be. Many people confuse them with rutabagas, which are orange or yellow, larger by far, and take forever to mature. Turnips are white and quick. White Lady is ready to eat in thirty-five days; Purple-Top White Globe takes about twice as long. Start harvesting turnips when they are golf-ball size; the flavor will amaze you. Sow turnip seed much like radish, but thin and thin again. First thin to 2 inches apart. Then take out every other one, and let the others grow larger. The greens are edible, but not a delicacy in my opinion.

Beets

Since beets store well, I wouldn't normally grow them in the greenhouse, but beet greens are much tastier than turnip greens. If you want to grow some, sow like spinach and thin several times, eating greens and baby beets. Better yet, buy the seed of beets that are grown only for their greens.

Onions

About the only kind of onions practical to grow in the home greenhouse are green onions, also called bunching onions or scallions. Technically, bunching onions are pulled before any bulb forms; scallions have a slight bulb. Start them from seed sown thickly; you probably wouldn't use sets anyway, but onion bulbs should never be brought into the greenhouse because they may have onion thrips, which will attack plants other than onions and can be almost impossible to eradicate if they get a start. Try White Lisbon or any other good bunching onion.

Other Cold-Weather Crops

Peas can be grown in the greenhouse, but they take up a great deal of space and cut off light, like any trellised vegetable, and home-frozen peas are nearly as delicious as greenhouse-grown ones. You might think that snow or snap peas would take less time, since you eat the pod, but that's not the case; some varieties of old-fashioned peas that need shelling are just as quick, maturing in about forty-five days. Peas might do better in very early spring than in fall; I've never grown them indoors.

Cabbage stores fairly well, but if you want some fresh, you can grow early cabbage like Primo indoors in large pots. It would take up less space than broccoli, Brussels sprouts, or cauliflower, all of which could conceivably be grown the same way, but all of which can be home frozen from summer garden crops.

Recent studies indicate that broccoli sprouts, easily grown in the greenhouse, offer more protection against cancer than any other food. If you want to try them, obtain directions for growing alfalfa or bean sprouts and follow them, but be *sure* that the seed is untreated and not pelletized when growing them or any other kind of sprouts (except Brussels, of course). Eating sprouts from treated seed could make you very ill; even pelletized seed contains materials that would probably find their way into the sprouts and be bad for the consumer.

WARM-WEATHER CROPS

Peppers, tomatoes, eggplant, and cucumbers share several characteristics. All are much better, and sometimes safer, homegrown than store-bought, especially if they come from outside the United States. Sometimes it's impossible to determine where supermarket produce did come from.

On the other hand, all are a lot harder to grow in the greenhouse than lettuce or chard. All take up space and light that other plants could use. Some need hand pollination to a greater or lesser degree. Because of light needs, all may do better started in very early spring (January 1) to mature in May or June than in fall.

Start seed for any of these in heated soil. Transplant, perhaps twice, ending with each plant in a 5-gallon pail (with drainage holes) or similar container. Give plants all the light and heat you possibly can, particularly for the first couple of months. It is possible to give them too much heat later on; some varieties of tomatoes will not set fruit if daytime highs approach 90.

Greenhouse Tomatoes

Tomatoes have always come in two kinds, determinate and indeterminate. Breeders have now developed a new kind, called ISI (indeterminate short internode), which are said to combine the best features of both. Determinate tomato plants grow until they are fair-sized bushes, then stop. Indeterminate ones are vines; they go on forever, until frost or something else stops them. Indeterminates need a lot of space and a lot of support in the greenhouse, but even determinates will probably need staking up.

Most greenhousers choose determinates, for space reasons, but many indoor gardeners find they have better luck with cherry or golf-ball-size tomatoes, even indeterminate ones, than with plants that are supposed to produce huge fruit.

Tiny Tim is a determinate cherry tomato plant that, at maturity, is only a bit more than a foot tall. Patio, as the name implies, can be grown on a deck or patio (as well as indoors) and produces medium-size fruit. Viva is an Italian plum type that I have found to be highly superior to the better-known Roma. It is resistant to many more diseases than Roma. Pixie is a popular hybrid determinate; its fruits are about twice the size of regular cherry tomatoes.

Sungold is a relatively new cherry tomato, yellow-orange when ripe. Many rave about its taste; we still prefer Sweet 100. Both are indetermi-

Fig. 74. Tomato.

nate. Ace and Homestead are popular determinate varieties that produce full-size fruit. Ace fruits are larger; Homestead can stand hotter conditions. Sunray is a disease-resistant yellow tomato that is relatively low in acid. Other tomato varieties are discussed in chapter 7.

Totally Tomatoes particularly recommends five tomatoes for greenhouse growth: Buffalo, Caruso, Dombito, Jumbo, and Tropic. These are all indeterminate hybrids, and most are either VF or VT resistant, or both. I have not tried any of them.

Stokes offers seed for about ten kinds of greenhouse forcing tomatoes. These are designed to be started about January 1 and transplanted March 15 for an early-summer crop or planted June 15 and transplanted in early July for a fall crop. In either case, the greenhouser would have to use artificial means to have daytime temperatures around 75 and nighttime ones about 65, and supplementary artificial light in January. These are designed for commercial growers; a packet contains more seeds than you would probably want and is relatively expensive.

Tomatoes must be pollinated; fortunately, insects aren't necessary for pollination. In the garden, wind does much of it. In the greenhouse, for best results, shake each blossom each day. You will get much better production if you do this around noon, or at least not in early morning or late evening. Believe it or not, small commercial growers use an electric toothbrush. Large ones use vibrators.

In addition to hand vibration or using a toothbrush, tomatoes can be pollinated, if they are on wire trellises, by vibrating the wire by rubbing it or striking it gently with a baseball bat or similar object. Peppers are pollinated much like tomatoes, although, even more than tomatoes, they sometimes seem to get pollinated without help from insect or man. Varieties of sweet and hot peppers are discussed in chapter 7.

Of the three common Solanaceae, tomatoes are the least trouble and eggplant the most, with peppers in the middle. Eggplants require more heat, both to germinate and to grow, and richer soil than tomatoes, and are the least easily pollinated. Sometimes simply shaking the plant is enough; with some varieties, or even some individuals, you may have to use an artist's brush, as with regular cucumbers and other cucurbits.

Cucumbers

You can grow ordinary garden cucumbers in your greenhouse, but unlike tomatoes, in the garden they require bees or other insects for pollination, so in the greenhouse you'll have to pollinate them individually and laboriously. Use an artist's paintbrush. Thrust it gently into a male blossom, twist a bit, then thrust it into a female blossom. Female blossoms have a tiny cuke behind them; males don't. Soon after a blossom has been successfully pollinated, it will wilt slightly; but that's a sign it doesn't need your services anymore. You will probably have more luck growing them in early spring, starting seed just after New Year's Day, than in late fall.

Or you can grow European cucumbers, the long, skinny kind that are said to be "burpless." I don't think they taste as good, but some of them are parthenocarpic, which means they need no pollination. In fact, if bees do get at the blossoms, they will produce monsters. These can be started in early January or early August, depending on whether you want very early or very late cucumbers, and require nights about 65 degrees and days of 72 or better. They will need artificial light in January and perhaps in late fall, and the price of the seed will take your breath away. Stokes offers eight varieties, with seeds costing 40 cents *apiece* or more, but these will probably do much better in the greenhouse than Straight Eight or Longfellow.

Whatever kind you grow, plan to grow them on a trellis, like pole beans. If you grow melons, squash, or indeterminate tomatoes, this will also be necessary. Since the trellis full of vines and fruit will block most of the light from whatever glazing is behind it, you'll need a large greenhouse, or a strong preference for these crops over homelier ones like lettuce or turnips. It's certainly possible and probably more practical to grow cold-weather crops like spinach and radishes in fall and warm-weather crops like tomatoes and beans in spring.

Beans

If you really think frozen beans don't compare with fresh, erect a trellis and grow a pole bean, such as Kentucky Wonder Wax or Scarlet Runner, in fall. Eremite is particularly recommended for greenhouses; the seed is expensive, like all seed specially designed for greenhouse growth, but you could save your own seed and have the expense only the first year. These beans mature in about fifty-five days and will provide eight or nine pickings of excellent long-podded beans over a three-week period. Beans do not require pollination.

Other Warm-Weather Crops

Melons and squashes of various kinds can be grown in the greenhouse, on trellises, with difficulty. Look for special small-bush varieties. These crops require paintbrush pollination, and when fruit is set, each ought to be supported in its own "hammock," usually made of pantyhose. I can't imagine growing pumpkins indoors, but somebody probably does.

CITRUS FRUIT

An orange is not a vegetable, a flower, or an herb, but you can grow citrus fruit in your greenhouse successfully, so we'll list it here with the vegetables. The easiest citrus to grow at home is the calamondin. The fruit looks and peels like a small tangerine. Some say calamondins have a pleasant tangy taste; we found ours quite sour, but they made great marmalade, especially with the addition of one or two lemons and navel oranges. The plant will have buds, blossoms, green fruit, and ripe fruit all at the same time. This dwarf shrub is not supposed to grow more than 2 feet high; ours was nearer 4 before we gave it away. The next best citrus to grow in the greenhouse is a lemon. The ones that produce a few huge, somewhat less sour fruit are ideal.

All such plants do very well in the home greenhouse, needing as much sun as you can possibly give them and a soil on the acid side that drains readily and contains plenty of humus. They should dry out completely between waterings. All citrus plants are subject to chlorosis, a yellowing of the leaves caused by iron deficiency or too high a soil pH, or both. The usual cure is to add iron chelate, available in garden supply stores, to the water given the plant.

It is unlikely that you can grow any citrus from seed; if you plant a seed from the hybrid orange you buy at the store, you'll almost certainly get a monster. Plants can be pruned and repotted, but sometimes this is a major operation with a very large plant. Buy another from a catalog supplier or grow one from a woody stem cutting.

Herb Crops

The majority of greenhousers don't grow vegetables in the greenhouse for consumption in the off-season, nor do they have banks of gladiolas or snapdragons to furnish cut flowers. Most of us, however, have a few pots, often quite a few pots, of herbs in the greenhouse all winter. Incidentally, pronounce it "herb" or "erb," as you wish; you will be correct either way, no matter what your snooty neighbor says.

Herbs are the ideal fall, spring, and winter greenhouse crop. It is difficult, to say the least, to grow enough potatoes in the home greenhouse to feed a family, but you can grow enough parsley, sage, rosemary, and thyme. You can freeze peas or store carrots. The usual way to preserve herbs is to dry them; however, with just a few exceptions, such as sweet woodruff, fresh herbs are better than dried. Some herbs, like parsley, basil, and chervil, are not usually dried because they lose just about all of their flavor. Dried parsley tastes exactly like hay–old, stale hay at that. At least, so I've been told; I've never tasted hay. Other herbs are usable dried but better fresh. Finally, some perennials will not winter over, at least not in Zone 4 or colder areas, and must be brought inside. Rosemary is a classic example.

With a few exceptions, herbs are easy to grow. Almost all do well in poor soil; some say that herbs grown in poor soil produce more and better essential oils, even though the plant may not grow as tall. Most herbs require nothing much beyond soil that drains well and plenty of light. Most need, at a minimum, five hours of sunlight, which is no problem unless you have a long cloudy spell in winter. Many, like oregano, grew naturally in a Mediterranean climate, one that is warm and wet in summer and cool and dry in winter, and will do very well in northern winter greenhouse conditions unless daytime temperatures are allowed to go too high. Assume these growing conditions for all herbs in the list that follows; exceptions will be noted.

Grow all herbs from seed unless otherwise noted. Cover small seeds lightly, larger ones to a depth of about twice their diameter. Many herb seeds, like basil, germinate readily; others have the reputation of being hard to grow.

Usually this is only because they take so long to germinate, and during that entire period the soil must be kept moist and warm. Some have poor germination percentages, but if you plant twenty-five rosemary seeds and only eight come up, you are still going to have enough rosemary.

Most herbs are resistant to insects and disease. Indeed, many herbs are suggested as companion plants to other crops in the garden because they repel insects. It seems, however, that no plant exists that has no enemies. Tobacco is an ingredient in insecticides, but some bugs thrive on a steady diet of tobacco.

Grow herbs in pots rather than beds; it makes bottom watering possible, and you may have to move specimens or throw them out. For all of them, use 6-inch or larger pots. Start seeds directly in pots or transplant. If you start in pots, plant three seeds in each pot and snip off all but the best seedling. Eat the thinnings; baby basil and parsley taste just like adult plants.

Put coarse gravel in the bottom of the pot, and use a soil mixture with somewhat more sand than normal. Use less fertilizer than you would with other crops. Don't make the mistake, however, of thinking herbs will thrive in totally unfertilized gravelly sand containing no humus.

Human beings have used herbs for healing for many millenia. There can be no question that some plants have medicinal qualities; quinine and digitalis are two plant-based compounds that are accepted by mainstream doctors. There is still much debate, however, about the medicinal use of many herbs. In the list that follows, culinary advice is guaranteed; medical advice is mostly of the "some say" variety. Be very conservative in the use of herbs to improve health; what is accepted wisdom today may be considered shockingly unwise tomorrow. For example, old books recommended rue for a variety of ailments; today's botanists and doctors consider it poisonous, if only mildly.

If you want maximum flavor or health benefits, pick fresh leaves early in the day. The herbs that follow are suitable for growing in the greenhouse.

ANNUALS

With all annuals, it is wise to plant a very few seeds, a half dozen or so, of each variety every two weeks. Many will grow too high if left alone for a couple of months, but you can start using them early and throw them out before they reach maturity. Unless you want the seeds, pinch off buds. This is particularly necessary with basil.

Basil

Basil is an ideal greenhouse plant, although some of our ancestors didn't think too much of it. Some thought it was a plant of the devil that would not grow unless the gardener screamed and swore while planting it. In some parts of France, "sowing the basil" means shouting and swearing. In general, it is unwise to move basil plants in from outdoors in the fall; you will almost always bring aphids in with them, and basil is easy to grow from seed.

Fig. 75. "Sowing the basil."

In addition to common basil, which will eventually grow awkwardly tall for the greenhouse, there is bush basil, a dwarf variety with tiny pointed leaves. Opal or purple basil is reddish purple. Lettuce-leaf basil has very large, curly leaves and grows well indoors. All of these taste about the same, but lemon basil, also a small plant, has a strong lemony flavor.

Fig. 76. Basil.

Basil and tomatoes are a standard combination, but basil is also good with peas and beans. Pesto is a basil-based sauce that is superb on pasta or with crackers as a snack.

Borage

Borage is a blue-flowered herb that grows larger than most others listed here, but it is one of my favorites. It is ridiculously easy to grow, and it can be cut back and kept within bounds. True, it isn't as useful as some herbs, but the flowers make a delicious edible garnish in just about any cool drink or can be used in salads. When a flower is perfectly ripe, the blue petal part and black center can be peeled from the green "backing," which doesn't taste good. It's easier than it sounds.

Borage leaves are reputed to soothe a scratchy throat. I've found them to work, probably because, like horehound, they have an odd flavor and texture that promotes the production of saliva. Eating borage is said to produce courage; young women in the Middle Ages tried to get suitors to eat it, hoping that it would give them the courage to pop the question.

In the garden, borage self-sows to the extent that it becomes a nuisance, so it's clearly easy to grow from seed. It will grow 3 feet high and sprawling, but it starts to bloom before reaching that size and can be kept cut back. Grow it in a very large pot.

Chamomile

Chamomile is hard to kill. It probably grows wild in your gravel drive or walk; crushed, it smells of pineapple. Shakespeare said, "The more it is trodden on the faster it grows," and he was right. Chamomile's tiny, daisylike flowers are pretty as well as useful, but there are two drawbacks to growing it in the greenhouse. The first is that the seed is fluff. When you open the package, you won't believe what you see. It is not hard to germinate, but you will wind up with a lot of tiny intertwined plants.

The second drawback is that chamomile tea, said to be a sedative and soothing to colds, is best made from the dried flowers. Since you can grow it outdoors in summer and dry it, you don't particularly need it fresh. Dried chamomile is also good in potpourri.

There are at least two different but extremely similar plants called chamomile: Roman chamomile (*Chamaemelum nobile*) and German chamomile (*Matricaria recutita*), which makes the best tea.

Chervil

Chervil is one of the exceptions: It thrives in shade and likes fairly moist conditions. Outdoors, it grows best under a bush; in the greenhouse, keep it in a darker location or make sure a larger plant shades it some of the time, and water it more frequently than you do most herbs. It is fairly hard to germinate, taking a long time, like parsley. It is said to be difficult to transplant, but I haven't found it so. It looks like parsley, only fernier, seldom grows very large or tall; and has the anise or licorice flavor shared by many herbs. You can't make béarnaise sauce without it. Dried chervil is very inferior to fresh.

Cilantro (Coriander)

Twenty years ago, almost nobody in America had ever heard of *cilantro*, which is what the plant and its leaves are usually called now, although many knew *coriander*, which is the name of its seed. In fact, I have a book not twenty years old that says, "The feathery leaves are not used in cooking."

It's not practical for most of us to harvest coriander seed indoors, as the plant grows too high before it goes to seed, but you can grow the plant for its leaves if you like their rather odd flavor. Grow it like any other herb, but plant it where it will live; its long taproot makes it well-nigh impossible to transplant. Use a deep pot. Cilantro, also known as Chinese parsley, is very unusual in that the first leaves—not just the seed leaves—but some thereafter, look like clover, but the later leaves resemble dill. These later ones are the leaves that are important in many ethnic cuisines, including those as disparate as Mexican and East Indian.

The fairly large seed germinates easily, and you will have no difficulty harvesting your own coriander seed from the garden and growing cilantro from it. Curiously, the round "seed" is actually two seeds. It will almost always produce two plants, but most growers don't thin them.

Dill

Dill is like cilantro in many ways—long taproot, too tall to grow for seed, feathery leaves—but it differs in that there are dwarf varieties that may provide seed before they are too tall for the greenhouse. Bouquet Dill grows less tall than Dukat; Fernleaf Dwarf at maturity is only 18 inches tall. Dill needs a deep pot. Dill seed is rather like parsnip seed, flat, round, and light in weight. It germinates easily, but it's hard to separate the seeds and get just one or two in each pot.

The flavor of dill is more popular with most Americans than that of cilantro; in Scandinavian countries, it is said that dill "is not an herb; it's a religious experience." It goes very well with salmon, in sour cream, and with cucumbers. The seed is essential for some pickles.

Marjoram and Oregano

Even expert plantsmen have difficulty telling the various oreganos and marjorams apart. The true ones are all *Origanum,* but in Mexico and the Caribbean, certain *Coleus* or *Lippia* varieties are called "oregano." I find it easiest to regard marjoram as annual oregano or oregano as perennial marjoram.

Marjoram is probably better to grow in the greenhouse than oregano, which will soon spread all over the place. Like many herbs, including basil, it is a mint. Follow growing directions for any herb. Use it in pizza or other Italian dishes.

Fig. 77. Marjoram.   *Fig. 78. Oregano.*

Summer Savory

Most Americans don't know the peppery flavor of summer savory, but it is very popular with our neighbors to the north and in German cooking. It is a particularly good complement to beans, either fresh or dried. Grow it much like dill, but it won't get quite so tall. Winter savory is a perennial that is quite similar to summer savory. Like all annuals, summer savory has the advantage of not cluttering up the greenhouse all year or needing to be moved outside. It is easy to grow from seed.

PERENNIALS AND BIENNIALS

If you grow perennial herbs in the greenhouse, it is best to set them out in the garden each spring for many reasons. It is also wise to start new plants every once in a while; many perennials, notably rosemary, mint, and thyme, will just up and die on you for no apparent reason.

Aloe

Immediately we have an exception to the above rule; don't ever put aloes into the garden. I wouldn't even put them outdoors in pots, as some do. Too much rainfall is bad for them. Aloes are propagated by division.

Another gardener will give you some; anyone who has aloes has too many. They are nearly impossible to kill, except by overwatering. A friend once cared for mine for a month. She must have watered them every day; when I got them back, they had terrible root rot. I unpotted them, actually washed the roots, threw some plants away, let the rest dry out completely, then potted them up in just about pure sand and gravel and went back to watering once a month or less. They did fine.

Fig. 79. Aloe.

Aloe vera ("true aloe"), as it is called, is said to be good for just about everything. It is an ingredient in many cosmetic creams; as such, it can't do any harm if you rub it on your face. I wouldn't take it internally, although the ancients did. One thing is definitely true about it. It helps greatly in the treatment of burns. Keep at least one pot near the kitchen stove; if you burn yourself, break off a piece and rub the juicy end on the burn repeatedly.

Bay

"The green bay tree" won't winter over in Zone 7 or lower and gets too big to move in and out, but it is a great greenhouse plant. If you have the right arrangement of deck and greenhouse, you can keep it in a pot on a wheeled dolly and wheel it out on the deck for the summer.

Historically, bay (*Laurus nobilis*) is the laurel of the ancients. Olympic winners were crowned with it, and it was sacred to Apollo.

Like all herbs, it was believed in the Middle Ages to cure practically everything, but it is little used medicinally today. It is, however, a wonderful addition, whole, to all kinds of soups and stews.

If you want a bay tree, it is probably easiest to purchase a young plant from a commercial grower. If a friend has one, you may be able to take a cutting, if you don't mind waiting half a year or more for it to root. Most gardeners have no luck starting it from seeds, which take a month to germinate. It likes about the same conditions as other herbs but will stand some shade.

Chives

Chives are one of the handiest herbs for greenhouse growth. Dried chives are right up there with dried parsley for tasting like hay, but you can take your scissors and snip from your pot of chives as many tips as you want for dip or other uses. Once you have a pot, it practically never dies. The attractive purple-blue blooms are edible in salad.

Chives are easy to grow from seed, but it takes a long time to get a really good pot of them that way. The plant is an allium, so it forms bulbs and divides, or should we say multiplies. If you plant a dozen seeds in a 6-inch pot, you should have enough in about two years. (This is one time you *don't* thin.)

You can buy a pot, or if you or a friend has mature chives growing outdoors, here's a clever trick: Divide a clump in fall and pot up enough of it for your needs. Leave the pot outside until several

Fig. 80. Chives.

severe frosts have killed all the apparent growth. Bring it in and water it, and lush new growth will appear. This not only provides you with the chives you need at once, but also kills off any possible insects, although chives are not subject much to insects or disease.

Clary Sage

Clary is a biennial sage that is grown like and can be used similarly to perennial sage, discussed below. Besides being biennial, it differs in another regard: Its blue or pink flowers (technically bracts, or leaves, like the red part of a poinsettia) are much prettier and more spectacular than regular sage blossoms. It is very easy to grow from seed, and it self-sows in the garden. Our ancestors used it as an eyewash (clary is a corruption of "clear-eye") and fried it up in fritters. You might try the latter.

Garlic Chives

Garlic chives, sometimes called Chinese chives, deserve to be better known. They are similar to chives, but the leaves are flat rather than round, the flavor is more garlicky, and the clusters of tiny, star-shaped, white flowers are infinitely more beautiful than chive blossoms. Grow it just like regular chives. Use it lavishly in place of garlic or chives; the flavor is more delicate than that of garlic.

Ginger

What's the good of having a greenhouse if you don't grow something exotic that your greenhouseless colleagues can't? Ginger won't survive outdoors except in the tropics, and it is much sought after for culinary use. It also definitely soothes an upset stomach and prevents, or helps prevent, seasickness.

You may be able to grow it from gingerroot sold in the supermarket, but it's probably safer and more certain to buy rhizomes (branching roots of plants, like iris, which spread out underground and send up new shoots) from a nursery or catalog. It is a real tropical plant, requiring at least some shade, well-drained soil kept moist, and fairly warm temperatures, although it will probably not die in your greenhouse if nights dip below 50 occasionally. It can even be put out on the deck in the summer.

What you eat is the root, plain or candied. After you've had the plant a year, pull it up and cut off all the root. Use what you want and replant the rest. It will do just fine with this treatment.

Horehound

Horehound seems old-fashioned nowadays, but it is still used in commercial cough medicines, although probably nobody still believes that it will heal the bite of a rabid dog, which is how it got its name.

It is very easy to grow and winters over in Zone 4 and above. It thrives naturally in dry, sandy vacant lots, so it shouldn't be very hard to grow in the greenhouse. It can be propagated by division or from seed. The seed is a bit tricky to germinate; specialists say it germinates best if there are wide fluctuations in temperature or if the seed is kept moist and held at a temperature just above freezing for a month. I find, however, that a few horehounds always germinate in my seed flat, sometimes long after everything else has been transplanted out of it.

If you want to make cough syrup in the wintertime, or just want to chew a bitter leaf when you have a tickle in the throat, raise it from seed or bring a plant or two in from the garden. It doesn't dry well. To make cough syrup, steep a teaspoon of fresh leaves in a cup of boiling water to make a tea. Mix the tea with twice as much honey, and take a teaspoon every four hours. It really helps.

Lavender

Lavender is used primarily for its scent, in potpourri or cosmetics. It is not hard to grow; the culture is much like that of rosemary, but lavender is much hardier. It is supposed to be difficult to get lavender seed to germinate, but my experience with it is exactly the same as with horehound. Lavender winters over readily in Zone 4 and is useful dried, but it's nice to have the scent of the fresh plant permeating the house in winter. Both leaves and blossoms can be used.

Lemon Balm

Lemon balm is often called just balm. It has a wonderful, lemony scent and a flavor that has been described as lemon with a hint of mint. It can be used in potpourri, as a tea of its own or in ordinary tea, and it is also pleasant rubbed on the hands or steamed to provide a facial.

It doesn't grow very tall, but it spreads like most mints. It's easy to raise from seed or division. The seed is said to require light to germinate, but if you cover it lightly, you'll probably get sufficient germination; if you don't, it's hard to keep it moist. One argument against growing it indoors in winter is that it dries very well, and the dried leaves are nearly as useful as the fresh ones.

Mint

There are dozens of kinds of mints. Most people are familiar with mint's flavor and culinary use, in a julep or with lamb. In our family, you can't make iced tea without it. Mint is also one of those herbs proven to have medicinal value, used to calm an upset stomach.

Mint is easy to grow and hard to get rid of. It can't be started from seed, but a friend will be glad to give you some. Its drawbacks, in addition to taking over the garden, include the fact that it cheerfully hybridizes, so you start

Fig. 81. Mint.

out with peppermint, spearmint, and chocolate mint and wind up with an amalgam of all three. Although it is said to repel aphids, it can be attractive to mites. Mint dries easily, but dried has nowhere near the flavor of fresh.

Parsley

If you didn't want to grow any other herb in the winter greenhouse, you'd probably want a pot or two of parsley. Everyone knows what it looks like and how it's used, but some don't know that though the prettier curled (French) parsley may be good for garnish, it is disdained by chefs in favor of the more flavorful flat leaf, or Italian, parsley. A variety from Italy, called Prezzemolo Gigante d'Italia, grows wide and high (for parsley) and has large leaves that have a really strong and sweet flavor. It is available from Pinetree Garden Seeds and perhaps elsewhere.

The difficulties of growing parsley and ways of overcoming them are discussed in

Fig. 82. Curly (French) parsley.

chapter 8, but remember that as a biennial, parsley will go to seed the second year. Often it doesn't produce many or tasty leaves that second year before going to seed, so it's good to start it afresh each year. Parsley really is good for you, containing lots of vitamins, and the chlorophyll in it sweetens your breath, so clean up that garnish on your plate. As a culinary herb, parsley not only has a wonderful flavor of its own, but also acts in concert with many other herbs to bring out their flavor.

Rosemary

My daughter in Georgia has a rosemary "tree" 4 feet high and very wide. I have to bring my little plants in every winter. In our part of Zone 4, tarragon and lavender will winter over easily. Rosemary, even if mulched heavily, usually will not. All my rosemary was started from seed. It has

slow, poor germination and takes a couple of years to grow to a decent size. If you have no luck with seed, you can raise it from cuttings you get from a friend. Grow it like all herbs, but water more sparingly than you do most. Although it seems immune to bugs and disease, more than any other plant in my experience, my rosemary plants seem always to just die, no matter what I do, so I start new plants every year.

An evergreen, rosemary is one of the most delightful and versatile of the culinary herbs. The needles are delicious with chicken, lamb, fish, beef, and veal. Try it with cheese or eggs, or in salad dressing. It even gives a wonderful scent to potpourris. But men beware: According to folklore rosemary thrives only where the woman "wears the pants in the family."

Fig. 83. Rosemary.

Sage

Sage is so popular in the Northeast as an ingredient in poultry stuffing that some call it "the New England herb." It is also blended into cheese and is used in sausage and in many other ways. It is easy to grow from seed, if the seed is fresh. Grow it like other herbs, but water it more than rosemary, at least until it is established. It is hardy as far north as many

Fig. 84. Sage.

parts of Canada, but old plants become woody and less useful, so it's a good idea to start some in the greenhouse every year.

Saint-John's-Wort

Saint-John's-wort is said to bloom on the birthday of John the Baptist. In earlier times it was thought to have all kinds of magic powers and to cure practically everything. A less charming old name for it is mugwort; it was used in ale. It is still widely prescribed in Europe as an antidepressant, being preferred there to drugs like Prozac, and is enjoying a vogue right now in the United States. Health food stores sell various pills and extracts containing the oil found in the leaves. Be careful, however; the Food and Drug Administration hasn't approved it as a medicine, and it can have very harmful side effects if overused.

Since it grows wild in woods and meadows all over the United States and Europe, except in the coldest parts, it can't be too hard to cultivate. You can dig one up in the woods, start seeds, divide a plant, or grow it from cuttings. It is happy with poor soil and bright sun or partial shade, but it wants a drink every once in a while. Although it is a perennial, it is short-lived at best, so start new plants every year.

Fig. 85. St.-John's-wort.

Tarragon

The true French tarragon (*Artemisia dracunculus*) can be grown only from cuttings or by division. Get a friend to give you a cutting or a piece of his big tarragon bush when he divides it, as he should every couple of years, or buy a plant. Russian tarragon is generally regarded as inferior for culinary purposes. This is not a political statement. Since the Latin name of Russian tarragon is *Artemisia dracunculoides,* it's not surprising that the two are just about indistinguishable in appearance. Growing conditions for tarragon are similar to those for most herbs, but it doesn't mind a rich soil.

Tarragon will winter over in Zone 4 and up, but grow some in the greenhouse to have it fresh for salad dressings and other uses. Like chervil, it has a slight licorice flavor, but the French couldn't cook without it. Use it sparingly in cooking, and add it when a dish is almost done; overcooking will make it bitter.

Thyme

There are probably more kinds of thyme than there are basils, sages, or mints, and there are plenty of those. Some are fairly upright, some crawling. Most taste more or less the same and are used extensively in cooking, in clam chowder, stews, barbecue sauce, and with hearty meat dishes. Dried thyme is almost as useful as fresh for these purposes.

Thyme will usually winter over in Zone 4 and above, although it may suffer some damage if not mulched. Since it grows well and easily indoors, there is no reason not to have a few pots in the greenhouse. I have had no difficulty starting it from seed; it can be grown equally well from cuttings. In the garden, the branches lean over, crawl along the ground, and root, so it's not hard to get new plants.

Fig. 86. Tarragon.

Fig. 87. Thyme.

Flower Crops

As with vegetables, you can grow any flowers you want to in the greenhouse. Some, however, are a good deal more practical than others. Flowering houseplants, such as African violets or Christmas cacti, are covered in chapter 12. This chapter deals with flowers that you might harvest in quantity, to decorate your tables and counters with fresh blooms, to take to a friend's home because she is ill or as a hostess gift, even, conceivably, to sell.

There is necessarily a great deal of arbitrariness about categorizing some flowers as houseplants and others as "cut flower" plants. Pansy blossoms make a beautiful display in a small, short vase or pitcher, and many a gardener has snipped off a leggy petunia and stuck it in a mixed bouquet. You don't have to be limited by the categories in this book; you can grow a few poppies as houseplants and a bed of petunias for cutting, if you wish.

ARTIFICIAL GROWTH TECHNIQUES

Many flowers have blooms that are triggered by external conditions, such as temperature or number of hours of daylight. For example, the large variety of marigolds will not bloom in the garden until the days start becoming short in mid-August or thereabouts. Florists have perfected techniques for fooling such plants. One way is to surround these marigolds with a dark box for part of a spring day to convince them that it is August. If you have the time, the inclination, and the equipment, you can try some of these tricks, but for the most part they are best left to commercial growers.

FORCING BULBS

One thing the home gardener can readily do is to force bulbs. Many think of bulb forcing as some esoteric activity that only experts can engage in, but it's fairly simple, once you think of it from the tulip or daffodil's point of view. When you plant tulips outdoors, you put bulbs in the ground fairly late in the year. They sometimes achieve a little root growth, but you don't want any shoots showing above ground for the winter to kill.

The bulbs undergo a period of dormancy under the ground and the snow. In our area, they experience severe cold, well below freezing, most winters. When the temperatures begin to rise, the plants begin to send up shoots. It doesn't have to get very warm by human standards; crocuses will shoot right up through a thin blanket of spring snow.

To force bulbs, all you have to do is convince them, first, that winter has come and, second, that spring is beginning to arrive. This is done after first potting them up. Bulbs that are forced must be in pots, not beds, either in pure gravel or pebbles or in potting soil. If the medium is not entirely gravel, the bottom third should be. The pots must have excellent drainage, or the bulbs will rot.

Put the bulbs in the medium right side up; you can usually see where roots have come out in the past, and the more pointed end is usually the top. Decide for yourself whether you want to grow one tulip in a small pot or a dozen daffodils in a lovely ceramic bowl, for giving away. Tulip bulbs have one side that is flatter; if you plant more than one tulip in a pot, place that side toward the rim. This will cause the leaves to drape more attractively over the rim. It is important that no two bulbs touch. Some growers cover all bulbs with an inch or two of medium; some do this with crocuses and irises but allow all others to have their noses showing.

Now convince the bulbs that winter has come and gone. First water the pots thoroughly; then place them in a cold, dark place. If you have a cellar, garage, or shed that is often 32 degrees but doesn't frequently go below 28, put them there and keep them dark. If temperatures don't get below 40 at night, the location is adequate, as long as they seldom rise above 45 in the daytime. Don't let them get bone dry; water occasionally and very sparingly. This is one place where the tepid water rule doesn't apply; water them with water as cold as they are.

If you don't have such a shed, you can achieve the same results by burying the pots a foot or two deep in a trench in a cold frame, or somewhat deeper in the garden, and covering them with something permeable to water like straw or cinders.

Some gardeners who force a good many bulbs buy an old clunker refrigerator and use it for nothing but chilling bulbs. Such refrigerators are often available from secondhand dealers for $50 to $100. They usually work well enough for the purpose, but be warned: Old refrigerators, especially those not in great shape, consume a good deal more electricity than the more efficient modern ones.

Leave bulbs in the cold, dark location about twelve weeks, thirteen minimum for tulips. If you can see roots beginning to appear out the holes in the bottom of the pot, they're "done." Now bring them into a warmer and lighter, but not too warm and light, place, such as an unheated, enclosed porch, and gradually accustom them to more heat and light. By now, shoots will be coming up. When, after a few days or a week, you move them into the full sun and heat of the greenhouse, they will grow astonishingly each day.

Bulbs are like seeds; they contain everything needed for the plant to get well started. Bulbs planted in nothing but gravel will usually flower beautifully, and the entire bowl with white gravel or stone chips and flowers makes a lovely gift. At some point, however, the plants need some nourishment, which is why plants you are going to keep, perhaps using the blooms as cut flowers, certainly reusing the bulbs, should be grown in a mixture of garden soil and a lighter commercial potting soil, with plenty of drainage. After the blossoms have appeared, the plants may be fertilized with a diluted solution of fish emulsion and a little bone meal, or a commercial bulb fertilizer if you are not an organic purist.

If you don't have a cold cellar, and burying pots outdoors—and digging them up when the ground is frozen and there's 3 feet of snow on the cold frame—seems like more work than it's worth, I'm with you. Stick to paperwhite narcissi. Buy them in a garden supply store or commercial greenhouse shortly before Thanksgiving, stick them in a pot, and don't fool around with any of that cold treatment stuff; just keep them as cool as possible at night. Give them to people for Christmas presents; the timing will be just right.

Fig. 88. Paperwhite narcissus.

Another bulb that can be purchased and forced without the necessity of chilling is amaryllis. These plants make an even more spectacular gift, with softball-size bulbs that produce blooms as large as 10 inches across. Put each bulb in a pot only 2 inches larger than itself, and let the top half show. Keep the medium moist, but not dripping. If the bulb seems reluctant, give it a shot of heat by putting a soil heater under it. It may be necessary to support the stalk.

FLOWERS FOR CUTTING

Flowers for cutting, even more than vegetables for harvest, will be grown in beds rather than pots, although there are exceptions. In general, start flower seeds and thin seedlings just as you would in the garden or for transplanting outside. You may want to start flowers where they are to grow, or transplant them from flats into beds once they have two true leaves. Most will need supports to grow straight and tall.

Most flowers take longer to come to maturity than most herbs or vegetables. Many commonly grown flowers take about three months

Fig. 89. A beautiful greenhouse bed made of brick, filled with zinnias.

under optimum conditions; some take much longer; few bloom in much less time.

Use the same soil conditioners and fertilizers that you would to grow the same flowers in the garden. Water as needed; use a device for measuring soil moisture, or just stick your finger well down in the soil. For most flowers, water only when the soil is bone dry, or nearly so. Remember these two facts: Plants grown using available sunlight in winter will take much longer to mature than it says on the seed packet, and plants receiving less sunlight and growing more slowly will need much less water than those out in the garden in July. Most flowers will do better if the greenhouse is on the cool side, especially at night. Exceptions are noted.

Listed here are a few, but by no means all, of the flowers that will produce blooms in the greenhouse in late fall, early spring, or winter. All are started from seed unless otherwise noted.

Ageratum

Although ageratum is usually thought of as a low-growing flower used outdoors in borders, there are varieties that grow 2 feet tall and produce the characteristic fuzzy blue or white blossoms. It takes three months or more from the planting of the seed until the blooms appear. Started in August, ageratum will usually be well acclimated when the lower-light conditions and cooler temperatures arrive and will bloom in late October or November. It doesn't mind occasional cool temperatures as long as they are well above freezing, but it will die or do poorly if the greenhouse gets too hot.

Bachelor's Button

You may know bachelor's buttons as cornflowers. If you can't find them in the seed catalog, look under *Centaurea*. Although they come in other colors, they characteristically have blue blossoms. There are many red and yellow but few blue flowers, which is one reason to grow them.

They will do well in a cool greenhouse, if soil is kept fairly dry. The 2-foot stems may need staking. It is important to deadhead them, and after the height of the blooming period, you should probably pull them up.

Fig. 90. Bachelor's button.

Calendula

A couple centuries ago, when writers referred to a "marigold," they meant what we now call the calendula or sometimes "pot marigold." Calendulas are among the best flowers for growing in the cool greenhouse and can be used as cut flowers or for their herbal qualities. Calendula provides an excellent yellow herbal dye. Medieval herbalists believed it would cure anything from toothache to stomach upset; most modern scientists are skeptical.

Fig. 91. Calendula.

Calendulas will bloom best if grown in heavier and more fertile soil than many greenhouse plants. Sow in July for October flowers, or in October for February blooms. Transplant about a foot apart. The best flowers will be produced if nighttime temperatures, after the plants are well started, dip into the 40s. Higher nighttime temperatures will produce more but smaller blooms.

Carnation

Carnations are usually grown from cuttings taken from garden plants in late fall but can be started from seed, which may produce smaller blooms. In either case, plants should be started in late fall. Carnations are slow growing and take quite a bit of care but are rewarding in appearance and scent. They can grow in soil with a wide pH range but like good drainage and a lot of phosphorus.

Either cuttings or seedlings should be transplanted into pots and repotted as they outgrow their surroundings; carnations do very poorly if potbound. They should be pinched back; like many plants, they will produce one showy bloom if other buds are removed. Too much watering is fatal to this plant.

Fig. 92. Carnation.

Chrysanthemum

Mums are hard to propagate. Most will not breed true from seed, and slipping is difficult, but a pot bought at a florist will last a long time if properly treated. Buy plants that are just budded, not ones in bloom. Inspect them, like all outsiders, very carefully, especially for aphids. *Don't* think plants from the florist can't be infested; they can, often without his knowledge. Quarantine them like all outsiders.

Alternatively, buy rooted cuttings, obtainable from many suppliers. Start them in spring and they will bloom in fall, but they must be kept in a *cool* spot. Blooms are many colors, usually shades of white, yellow, or brown. If not grown inside or brought into the greenhouse in fall, they will probably be winter-killed.

Gardenia

Call gardenias Cape jasmine, a name that suggests the fragrance, if you don't like Latin. They are among the sweetest-smelling flowers you can grow, and they're not too difficult to cultivate in the greenhouse, since they like lots of sun and cool, but not cold, nights. Gardenias, like citrus, need soil that is quite acid. The soil they are grown in can become more alkaline with repeated waterings, causing leaf chlorosis (pale leaves with dark veins). The standard cure is to add iron chelate to the water.

Gardenias can be put outdoors in light shade in summer, in a pot set into the garden. They are propagated from stem cuttings. Though they are not hard to grow, they are hard to get to bloom. They must have a minimum of four hours of sunlight a day; it may be necessary to supplement with artificial light. They need to be in moist but not waterlogged soil, in a humid atmosphere, and to be fed with an acid liquid fertilizer once a month.

Lupine

Annual lupines, whether pink or blue, are suitable for growing in the greenhouse. They need rich soil with plenty of humus and, like pincushion flowers, don't do well in even slightly acid soil. They can be started from seed where they are to grow or transplanted but should eventually be a foot apart. Lupines like nighttime temperatures in the low 50s.

Marigold

Marigolds are oddly unpopular with many gardeners, and even many of those who put them in the garden as bug repellers wouldn't dream of

Fig. 93. Marigold.

growing them as cut flowers, but they make great ones, especially if you don't want to do a lot of fussy work. It's true that the scent is not that of gardenias, and some regard the blooms as coarse looking, but that's a matter of taste. Most gardeners don't realize that the scent comes primarily from the foliage, not the blossoms. If the leaves are undisturbed, there will be much less aroma.

Sow the seeds of dwarf marigolds any time; choose from an array of colors, from light yellow through brownish red, and a variety of blossom types. If you sow them in early August, you'll have blooms in mid-October. Give them as much sun as possible, don't leave dead blossoms on the plant, and don't crowd them together. One expert says that spider mites like them, but I've never known anything except a deer to eat a marigold, and that was not in a greenhouse.

Tall marigolds are African; dwarf marigolds are French or French-African crosses. I don't recommend growing African marigolds indoors. It's true that they will provide cut flowers with longer stems, but they are light-sensitive like poinsettias and other plants, and to get them to blossom, you'll have to go to a lot of work to fool them into thinking it's late summer or fall.

Pincushion Flower

Pincushion flowers are also known as pincushion plants, scabious, or the Latin *Scabiosa*. Everybody ought to grow something old-fashioned, something sweet-smelling, something interesting, and something hard to grow. This is all of those things. Interesting? The flowers look exactly like pincushions, complete with pins stuck in them. The seeds look like tiny shuttlecocks from a badminton game. Pincushion flowers are very fragrant and

Fig. 94. Pincushion flower.

range in color from pink and red through purple to white. Our grandmothers knew them well.

As for difficult, they take a full six months from seed planting to bloom, possibly longer in the greenhouse. Start them in September for possible February or March bloom. They like rich soil that drains thoroughly and prefer a pH *above* 7.

Poppy

Poppies need quite a bit of room but can be grown indoors as cut flowers. Stick to Shirley or Iceland poppies; the legal status of the opium poppy (*Papaver somniferum*) and its close relatives is far from clear. Iceland poppies grow to be about a foot tall, about half as high as Shirleys. Both come in a wide variety of colors and blossom types.

Sow seed where the plant is to grow. Poppy seeds are tiny and hard to handle; you will probably need to thin considerably. Poppies can be transplanted, but it is quite difficult. After thinning, the plants should be 9 inches apart. Plant in early fall for a spring bloom. Poppies will do well in the cool conditions of the winter greenhouse if they get enough bright sun and soil is allowed to dry out between waterings. If you don't cut them for bouquets, remove dying flowers and seedpods.

Snapdragon

If you don't grow any other flowers in the greenhouse, grow snapdragons. Snaps come in many colors and are ideally suited for the production of cut flowers in the greenhouse. They will tolerate considerable cold and thrive in almost any soil. Sow in August for late winter or early-spring bloom; transplant to 10 inches apart. The tiny seeds make it difficult to produce one plant per cell, but the seedlings will stand some abuse in separation.

Try to obtain seeds of plants designed for greenhouse growing; you may have to shop around. Ordinary outdoor snapdragons may produce leaves but no blossoms. The seeds you want are sold as "winter-growing" or "greenhouse" types.

Snaps do better if pinched back when they are 3 to 4 inches high.

Stock

Stocks are wonderful old-fashioned flowers that are a good greenhouse source of cut blooms. They range in color from pink through lavender.

Like many other flowers of yesterday, they have a lovely scent. A greenhouse full of flowers in winter really ought to delight the nose as well as the eye.

Sow seeds in August. Transplant into beds, leaving about 8 inches between plants. Pinch back as with snapdragons. Stocks like a light, well-drained, but rich soil and very cool temperatures. If treated as described, they should bloom about late February.

Zinnia

Zinnias can be grown in the greenhouse, but they don't like cold, especially in their early stages. Other than that, they are among the least delicate of flowers, both in their requirements and in their appearance, which is why some turn up their noses at them. About their only other problem is a tendency to mildew, which can be averted to a considerable degree by not splashing the leaves when watering, a good practice in watering anything.

Fig. 95. Zinnia.

They come in many varieties and colors. Some varieties grow less than a foot high, others more than a yard. Some may bloom in as few as seventy-five days. The first zinnia was orange-yellow in color; now they come in just about anything but blue. Some will produce more blooms after the first are cut.

PART V

Ancillary Uses
for the Greenhouse

Other Uses
for a Greenhouse

The primary purpose of a greenhouse, as the name implies, is the growing of green things. The human animal, however, is incapable of having an area in its den that is dedicated to merely one activity. Kitchens double as dining rooms, and living rooms become entertainment centers. The electric trains find a permanent home in the spare bedroom, so that on the rare occasions when Aunt Sylvia visits, she has to share her room with a model of a Delaware Lackawanna 4-8-4. Greenhouses, too, evolve into centers for other activity. This evolution can take one of two forms—upward, as into a social center, or downward, as into a toolshed.

TOOLSHED OR STORAGE SHED

A freestanding greenhouse, which is not usually suitable for human habitation in the winter, often evolves into a toolshed. One gardener I know simply extended his greenhouse, partitioned off the end, and covered the roof and walls, not with glass, but with opaque material. He keeps lawn mowers, carts, rakes, and other tools in there, summer and winter (see fig. 1). Many another gardener finds that the spading forks and shovels wind up wintering over in the greenhouse without his volition.

It goes without saying that peat moss, gravel, potting soil, and similar materials are stored in any greenhouse, attached or freestanding. Where else would you store them? There is no other place as convenient to store plant pots, six-packs, and other containers in which to start or continue plants. Hand tools like trowels, dibbles, and pruning shears are often stored there as well.

There are some things that often wind up in the greenhouse that might better be kept elsewhere. Unless you have added a toolshed to a freestanding greenhouse, as described above, it's not a good idea to store large tools, like rakes and shovels, in it, and it's a very poor place in which to keep lawn mowers, hoses, wheelbarrows, and similar large items. In an attached greenhouse, it is, or should be, out of the question; most of us use attached greenhouses all winter, or pass through them to go outside, and constantly tripping or climbing over such items is a terrible nuisance.

CAUTION: Gasoline-powered equipment, like power mowers, or gasoline itself should NEVER be stored in an attached greenhouse or any other building attached to the house. Short of smoking in bed, doing so is one of the very best ways to burn your house down with you in it. Unless you have an attached garage that is suitably separated by fireproofing from the rest of the house, all such material should be kept in an outbuilding. That way, only the outbuilding goes up in flames. Gasoline-powered tools could be kept in a freestanding greenhouse if there is no better place available, since if it goes up in flames nothing living (except plants) will be lost, but bear in mind that such buildings may get very hot inside in the daytime as early as late February.

Seeds should be kept cool, dry, and dark, and since the greenhouse is generally hot, wet, and light, it is the worst possible place for their storage. Bulbs that are being wintered or summered over belong, like the seeds, in a cellar, if it is the rare cellar that's dry, or in the attic, if it's the rare attic that's cool without falling below freezing. Wherever they are kept, it shouldn't be the greenhouse.

MUDROOM

Probably the most common use of an attached greenhouse, particularly in the cold and wet months, is as a "mudroom." Mudrooms appear to be unknown in warm climes, but every old farmhouse in the North Country had its mudroom, where the farmer dropped his snowy, muddy, or even manury boots, jacket, gloves, and frequently other items of apparel, nearly down to the buff.

An attached greenhouse almost always has a door to the outdoors and a door into the rest of the house. It almost always has a floor made of brick, slate, or similar material and often has a water tap, sometimes a sink. It would be nice if we did not clutter up our greenhouses with muddy boots or snowy mittens, but about the only way to avoid it is to

Fig. 96. Greenhouse used as a mudroom.

construct another room with similar characteristics and insist on its being used as the mudroom, and that isn't possible for most of us. It is possible, and desirable, to provide pegs for jackets, bins for the storage of potting soil, and drawers for tools, and to line up muddy boots neatly.

FISHPOND

A much more exotic use of a freestanding greenhouse involves fish. A man I know grows bamboo all winter in a greenhouse that stands in his garden. There is minimal heat; the temperature occasionally drops below freezing, but not often, and not far. About one-third of the floor of this house is taken up with a carp pond. In winter, the fish are somnolent, but the cool, sometimes cold, temperatures do them no harm. The water in the pond is circulated through 30-gallon drums that also store solar energy; fish by-products are screened out and help fertilize the plants. Altogether, he has a miniature "Ark" or biosphere.

DRYING BULBS AND TUBERS

The greenhouse is the ideal place for drying bulbs and other plant materials before storing them elsewhere. Members of the onion family, for example, including garlic and shallots, can be dried for a few days in sunny areas of the greenhouse before they are stored. The usual recommendation for all onions is to dig them, when they are totally mature and the tops have dried, just before a few sunny days, and leave them in the garden for those days. Then inspect them for thrips, and bring them into the greenhouse for a week or two before storing them in a dark, cool place. If the weather forecast turns out to be wrong, adapt as best you can.

The greenhouse is also a good place to dry the potato crop before storage, but the tubers should be dried out of direct sunlight. Gardening books suggest not leaving potatoes exposed to sunlight for too long, but it is better not to expose the tubers to sun at all. Tubers or parts of tubers that are exposed to the sun and turn green should not be eaten.

It is probably worth mentioning in passing that I have never succeeded in drying plum tomatoes just by exposing them to sunlight in the greenhouse. No matter how hot and dry it is, mold always forms before they are sufficiently dry. This perhaps explains why every recipe I have found for sun-dried tomatoes instructs you to "sun-dry" them in the oven or microwave. We bought one of those low-heat food dryers.

DRYING HERBS

The greenhouse can also be used for the drying of herbs. I have never found a better way to dry herbs than this: Pick herbs fairly early in the morning, but after most of the dew has dried. Cut off stalks or seedheads with a pruner or garden scissors. *Don't* attempt to separate seeds or leaves from stalks at this point; put entire heads or stalks cut short enough to fit into a large brown paper bag. Cramming is OK. Close the neck of the bag and tie it with string, leaving a couple of feet of string attached. Label the bag; you'd be surprised how hard it may be later to tell, for example, dill seed from caraway.

Tie the bags to small finish nails driven a short distance into the upper frame of the window, and let them hang in the sunlight. Since you do this in late summer or fall, the fact that they block the light is a plus, not a minus. The bags need little support; the nails can be very small and driven in only a short way. They will be inconspicuous at other times of the year and do minimal damage to the frames. If the window frames in your greenhouse are metal, you'll have to improvise; masking tape might do.

Fig. 97. Drying herbs in bags in the greenhouse window.

Usually, two to three weeks is enough time to dry the herbs, but if you're like me, you won't get around to the next step until winter, when other gardening chores are at a minimum. The herbs might be slightly better if tackled earlier, but even if left three months, they'll be all right.

Separating the dried leaves or seeds from the chaff is a real pain, nor can this book give specific directions, because every herb is different. Round seeds like coriander will roll away from the chaff along creases in paper. They'll also roll into a lot of places you don't want them to.

In some cases, the part you want, like dill seed, is denser than the part you don't want. Supposedly, primitive peoples separated good corn from chaff by dropping the material 6 feet or so onto a blanket outdoors when a gentle breeze was blowing. This has never worked well for me, but I have found that if I put the material into a large glass bowl and blow on it with the right amount of force, most of the chaff leaves the bowl and most of the good stuff remains behind. The operative word here is *most*.

These two thoughts may help: You're getting these dried herbs free; check the prices in the store. And you're not selling the finished product, but using it yourself or giving it away. Presumably you, or your friends, can cope with the odd bit of stick or dried spider. By the same token, if a few good bits get into the chaff, *throw them away!* You didn't pay for them anyway. If you do plan to sell home-dried herbs, you'll have to find out what state laws say about that. Chances are that after consulting them you'll change your mind.

SOCIAL CENTER

There is one problem with attached greenhouses that I have never solved. There are exceptions, but the typical attached greenhouse, like mine, has these characteristics: It takes up a considerable part of the south side of the house. It is connected to some other room, often a living room, with glass doors. The best view from the house, especially if it is a solar house, is to the south.

This means that, ideally, guests could sit in your living room and look out over the fields and woods, perhaps to a lake or distant mountains, through your greenhouse. It doesn't usually work that way. Instead, your guests are looking into a jumble of tools, bags of peat moss, and muddy boots, possibly tempered by a collection of beautiful plants. This problem is obviously solvable by keeping the peat moss and muddy boots else-

Fig. 98. An exotic but pleasant ancillary use of a greenhouse.

where, but as I said, most of us have never solved it, except by having guests after dark and keeping the lights out in the greenhouse.

We do know someone who has a hot tub in the greenhouse, and we are sure there are others. There are a number of advantages to this arrangement. The heat of the greenhouse in the daytime helps keep the water in the hot tub warm, and the warm water helps moderate the night-time temperature in the greenhouse. The water in the hot tub has to have an external source of heat, which can come from solar panels on the south-facing greenhouse roof, if it isn't totally glass. The presence of the hot tub also helps increase humidity in the greenhouse. Especially in winter, greenhouses are seldom humid enough to provide an ideal atmosphere for the plants they contain.

Some books show bathrooms that appear to be miniature greenhouses. These rooms would provide the humidity desired, but it would be hard to use one as a working greenhouse in which to start a flat of onions, and for most of us it would be difficult to entertain guests in such a room.

The final advantage of the hot tub we are familiar with—the old-fashioned round wooden one—is that the people inside it tend not to look at the muddy garments or bags of potting soil outside it, but instead at one another or the plants hanging overhead.

It is, of course, possible to have your greenhouse or conservatory be the most beautiful and elegant room in your house. There are books, usually written by beautiful and elegant ladies, that tell us how to do that. Such rooms feature wrought iron chairs and tables with glass tops, with fernery and similar plants draped behind the guests' necks. If you are a beautiful and elegant lady, you can undoubtedly figure out how to create and maintain such a room, but if you're not, that's just one more thing I can't help you with.

Sources

Listed below are companies that sell seeds, plants, tools, organic pesticides, gardening gadgets, or ancillary products, such as worms. There may be five hundred seed companies in the United States and many in other countries. Omission from this list does not constitute lack of endorsement by Stackpole Books or the author, nor does inclusion denote endorsement.

SEED COMPANIES

Companies that sell seeds often offer many ancillary products. Almost every seed company has its own house varieties that no one else offers. Most seed companies have a toll-free fax number for orders only but a regular telephone number for everything else. I have not included these fax numbers, since you can't send an order until you have seen a catalog.

Bentley Seeds, Inc., 16 Railroad Ave., Cambridge, NY 12816, (518) 677-2603. Long ago, Cambridge, a small town in upstate eastern New York, was a center for seed growing. Bentley and Rice, listed below, are the remaining vestiges. Bentley, which sells all over the United States, is somewhat larger and quite a bit younger than Rice; otherwise, everything said about Rice, below, applies to Bentley.

Charles C. Hart Seed Company, P.O. Box 9169, 304 Main St., Wethersfield, CT 06129, (800)326-HART (4278). This company has been owned and operated by the Hart family for more than 100 years. The third, fourth, and fifth generations are currently active in the business. Hart specializes in fertilizers and vegetable and flower seeds for the home gardener.

Johnny's Selected Seeds, Foss Hill Rd., Albion, ME 04910-9731, (207) 437-4301. Johnny's is a small Maine company that sells mostly to home gardeners. It has varieties that are heirlooms or that do well in the North or both Its catalog probably gives more useful information than any other.

George W. Park Seed Co., Inc., 1 Parkton Ave., Greenwood, SC 29647-0001, (800)845-3369. Park's is a big, old seed company that lists far more flowers than vegetables in its large, colorful catalog. Most of its seeds come only in packets, which is a sign that it caters to home gardeners. I know from experience that if a customer feels that the company has made a mistake, it will go to any length to make things right.

Pinetree Garden Seeds, Box 300, New Gloucester, ME 04260, (207) 926-3400. Pinetree is another small Maine company, a trifle younger and probably smaller than Johnny's. It offers a nonglossy catalog with few photos and appears to be aimed at experienced hobby gardeners. All seeds are sold in packets only. Prices are quite low, but sometimes it's a surprise to see how few seeds are in a packet, until you realize that (a) you really don't need to start more than eighteen Better Boy tomatoes or one hundred Utah celery, and (b) the catalog told you approximately how many seeds you would receive. Pinetree has many European and Asian varieties that other companies don't.

Rice Seed Company, Inc., P.O. Box 69, Cambridge, NY 12816, (800) 224-RICE (7423). If you want to do business with a really old, tiny mom-and-pop seed company, call or write to Rice. The company is in its 165th year of continuous operation. It sells packets designed for home gardeners, mostly to be retailed by small hardware and similar stores in the northeastern United States, but it will sell direct to you upon request. Rice has lots of heirlooms; one of the owners told me that this was mostly because they started selling these varieties back in 1835 and never stopped. They stock no treated seed and very few hybrids; almost all Rice varieties are open-pollinated. All packets, except a very few containing more than one ounce, are the same (low) price.

Shepherds Garden Seeds, 30 Irene St., Torrington, CT 06790-6658, (860) 482-3638. Shepherds is an upscale seed company that offers seeds for many unusual European, Latin American, and Asian plants. It was recently purchased by White Flower Farm of Litchfield, CT.

R. H. Shumway, Seedsman, P.O. Box 1, Graniteville, SC 29829, (803) 663-9771. Shumway's is another big, old southern seed company; both Shumway's and Park's are well over one hundred years old. Shumway's advertises that it specializes in "Good Seeds Cheap." You won't find mesclun or bok choy in its catalog, but you will find Jerusalem artichokes and a wide variety of beans for drying. Shumway's is a whole or part owner of Totally Tomatoes. Vermont Bean Seed Company is entirely owned by Shumway's.

Stokes Seeds, Inc., Box 548, Buffalo, NY 14240-0548, (716) 695-6980. Stokes is a Canadian-American company; as such, it has a good supply of seeds intended for growing in cold climates. Stokes sells extensively to farmers as well as hobby gardeners and is one of the few companies that lists in its regular catalog a large number of varieties bred exclusively for greenhouse growth.

Totally Tomatoes, P.O. Box 1626, Augusta, GA 30903, (803) 663-0016. Totally Tomatoes sells seeds for nearly three hundred kinds of tomatoes, as well as about a hundred peppers and a few related plants like tomatillos.

OTHER PLANT SUPPLIERS

Wayside Gardens, Hodges, SC 29695-0001, (800) 845-1124. Wayside sells no seeds, but bulbs, shrubs, and plants of every imaginable kind, in pots or bare-rooted.

GARDEN-RELATED PRODUCTS

Gardens Alive!, 5100 Schenley Place, Lawrenceburg, IN 47025, (812) 537-8650. This is an excellent source of all kinds of organic fertilizers, pesticides, and similar materials. Gardens Alive! sells no seeds, but it does sell rotenone and pyrethrins, and even sulfur and copper compounds, which are said to be "organic." It is nonetheless one of the best sources of ladybugs, Bt's, good nematodes, sticky yellow bug traps, and other recommended controls.

Unco Industries, Inc., 7802 Old Spring St., Racine, WI 53406, and The Worm Connection, 581 Camino Manzanas, Thousand Oaks, CA 91360. You can buy worms and worm-composting-related products from these two suppliers.

Index